The Indestructible Woman in
Faulkner, Hemingway, and Steinbeck

Studies in Modern Literature, No. 45

A. Walton Litz, General Series Editor

Professor of English
Princeton University

Linda Wagner

Consulting Editor for Titles on Ernest Hemingway
Professor of English
Michigan State University

Thomas C. Moser

Consulting Editor for Titles on Joseph Conrad
Professor of English
Stanford University

Other Titles in This Series

The Indestructible Woman in
Faulkner, Hemingway, and Steinbeck

by
Mimi Reisel Gladstein

U·M·I Research Press

Ann Arbor / London

Produced and distributed by
UMI Research Press
an imprint of
University Microfilms Inc.
Ann Arbor, Michigan 48106

Library of Congress Cataloging in Publication Data

Gladstein, Mimi Reisel.
The indestructible woman in Faulkner, Hemingway,
and Steinbeck.

(Studies in modern literature ; no. 45)
Revision òf thesis (Ph.D.)—University of New Mexico,
1973.
Bibliography: p.
Includes index.
1. American fiction—20th century—History and
criticism.   2. American fiction—Men authors—History
and criticism.   3. Women in literature.   4. Sex role
in literature.   5. Faulkner, William, 1897-1962—
Characters—Women.   6. Hemingway, Ernest, 1899-1961—
Characters—Women.   7. Steinbeck, John, 1902-1968—
Characters—Women.   I. Title.   II. Series.
PS374.W6G55   1986   813'.52'09352042   86-4296
ISBN 0-8357-1662-7 (alk. paper)

For the women whose love and strengths enrich my life:
Gaga, Denise, Holli,
Nettie, Beth, Debby, Sally,
Sharon, Karen, Davette, and Tobi

Contents

Abbreviations

All references to primary sources will be abbreviated in the text. The following abbreviations will be used:

Faulkner

A,A!:	*Absalom, Absalom!*
AILD:	*As I Lay Dying*
H:	*The Hamlet*
IITD:	*Intruder in the Dust*
LIA:	*Light in August*
M:	*The Mansion*
S:	*Sanctuary*
Sar:	*Sartoris*
SF:	*The Sound and the Fury*
T:	*The Town*
U:	*The Unvanquished*

Hemingway

ARIT:	*Across the River and into the Trees*
FWBT:	*For Whom the Bell Tolls*
MF:	*A Moveable Feast*
OMAS:	*The Old Man and the Sea*
SAR:	*The Sun Also Rises*
SSOEH:	*The Short Stories of Ernest Hemingway*

Steinbeck

BB:	*Burning Bright*
EE:	*East of Eden*

GW:	*The Grapes of Wrath*
LV:	*The Long Valley*
PH:	*The Pastures of Heaven*
P:	*The Pearl*
ST:	*Sweet Thursday*
TGU:	*To a God Unknown*

Preface

The first version of this study was completed in 1973. Since that time the MLA index lists as having been published close to 2000 items on Faulkner, approximately 1500 on Hemingway, and about 350 on Steinbeck. Faulkner's women are the most numerous and the writing about them reflects that. I have attempted to incorporate much of the new research in both my text and notes. Attendance at the 1985 "Faulkner and Yoknapatawpha" conference on Faulkner and Women was especially helpful. Joseph Blotner's new one-volume edition of *Faulkner: A Biography* provided new materials that helped verify certain biographical and psychological readings of Faulkner's depiction of women. Although there has always seemed to be a surplus of biographical and critical readings of Hemingway, the publication of several new works has enhanced this study. In some cases they have merely validated readings that I originally predicated on speculation; in other cases they have provided important new information. Bernice Kert's *The Hemingway Women* and Scott Donaldson's *By Force of Will* present new information and readings that make significant contributions to the study of Hemingway's fictional depiction of women. All Steinbeck scholars are in debt to Jackson J. Benson for his mammoth biography *The True Adventures of John Steinbeck, Writer*. He has given us all a resource rich in detail and interpretation. Benson shows a sensitivity to the question of Steinbeck's relationships with women which has been missing in previous biographical studies. The Steinbeck Monograph Series monograph *Steinbeck's Women: Essays in Criticism* edited by Tetsumaro Hayashi is another helpful work.

I am concerned that this work might somehow be interpreted as demonstrating that Faulkner, Hemingway, and Steinbeck were nascent feminists because of their depiction of such strong and indomitable women. Nothing could be further from my purpose. Both in their personal relationships and in their fictional depictions of women, they all three exhibited chauvinistic and sexist traits. If anything, the indestructible woman is a projection of that sexism. According to one dictionary definition, sexism is an attitude that promotes stereotyping based on gender, which is exactly what these authors are doing in their depiction of the indestructibility of women. However, neither do I want this study to be read as a condemnation of these three because of their sexism. They were children of their times and, if anything, should be commended for their occasional attempts to transcend traditional frames of reference. I, who am some two generations younger than any of these men, remember that my own attitudes toward women had to undergo considerable consciousness-raising in the sixties. They did not have the benefit of that experience.

Acknowledgments

My thanks again to the late Hoyt Trowbridge, Bob Fleming, and David Jones of the University of New Mexico for their direction of the original version of this study. John and Flo Dick also provided invaluable aid at that time, as did my husband Jay, my children Cliff, Denise, and Alfie, and my sister Holli Berry. My father Emil Reisel, since deceased, and my mother Regina Reisel have been bulwarks throughout my life.

A reduced teaching load to work on the revision of this study was provided by Diana Natalicio, dean of liberal arts at the University of Texas at El Paso. Thanks are due Tetsumaro Hayashi for permission to reprint portions of this work which were first published in slightly altered form in the *Steinbeck Quarterly*. Professor Hayashi's encouragement and support of my studies in Steinbeck are greatly appreciated. Evans Harrington, Ann Abadie, and Doreen Fowler have permitted me to print portions of this study which are also being published in *Faulkner and Women: Faulkner and Yoknapatawpha 1985*. My thanks to Gail Mortimer who read a portion of the Faulkner chapter and suggested some helpful revisions. Helen Bell of the University of Texas at El Paso library was helpful, as she always is, in locating and securing new materials.

1

Introduction

Anyone who has been reading literary criticism in this generation is aware that American male novelists have been accused, indicted, and convicted for the many failures in their depiction of women. The accusers are many. Their indictments are sweeping. Whether the forum be popular news magazines or feminist rereadings of American fiction, the general consensus is that the accused are guilty as charged. *Time* magazine, in a special issue on "The American Woman" declares, "Oddly women characters have never had a particularly important place in American literature...."[1] Negative stereotyping of women and girls in children's books is the cause of Diane Gersoni Stavn's concern. In a *Library Journal* article she decries the fact that even the good writers "seem limited in their ability to convincingly handle sexually and intellectually emancipated, real late-adolescent females."[2] The aptness of Carolyn Heilbrun's description of "the masculine wilderness of the American novel" has not been effectively challenged. Heilbrun remonstrates against the "male-fantasy novel that forms the mainstream of U.S. fiction...[and its] refusal to allow full humanity to women."[3] According to Heilbrun, "America, alone among nations of high culture, has been in its novels as in its life the celebrator of the 'manly' virtues of aggressiveness and violence, the great relegator of women to a place outside the meaningful life."[4] Judith Fetterley is no less emphatic. "American literature is male," she states. "Our literature neither leaves women alone nor allows them to participate. It insists on its universality at the same time that it defines that universality in specifically male terms."[5]

Most of this criticism comes in the wake of the women's liberation movement and much of it follows the pattern set by Kate Millett in *Sexual Politics*.[6] Millett sees misogynist literature as a primary vehicle of masculine hostility. Though this literature has a strong historical tradition, Millett points out that in the twentieth century, with the abatement of censorship, there has been a new frankness in expressing this hostility in specifically sexual contexts. The explicit portrayal of the degrading and insulting sexual exploitation of women, which was once forbidden outside pornography, is now given free expression, a development with obvious antisocial implications. In her landmark study, Millett first sets up the historical and ideological background for sexual politics, and then turns to a thorough roasting of those whom she sees as the architects of the sexist structure, the writers who as cultural agents reflect and shape attitudes. The main objects of her vituperation are D.H. Lawrence, Henry Miller, and Norman Mailer, the latter two Americans.

The list of feminist critics who have revisioned American literature and found it wanting in its portrayal of women is impressive.[7] But, though these attacks have become a critical commonplace and are now most often associated with feminist criticism, they were anticipated in Leslie Fiedler's *Love and Death in the American Novel* (1960), which was published nearly a decade before the first great wave of feminist literary scholarship. Fiedler indicts American male novelists' deficiencies in the characterization of women as well as their inabilities in depicting mature sexuality: "The Reign of Sentimentalism in the American novel not only made it exceedingly difficult for our writers to portray sexual passion, but it prevented them as well from drawing convincing portraits of women."[8] Fiedler's explanation of the reason for this deficiency is in keeping with the concept of the *otherness* of woman as defined in Simone de Beauvoir's *The Second Sex*, which was published in this country some seven years before his book was published.[9] In brief, the concept of *other*, which sees man as subject and woman as object, has strong roots in the story of Genesis and the Judeo-Christian ethic, the dominant theology in our culture. In the mythology of the Christian West and therefore of the American mind, woman was created, not as a separate, unique entity, but from the body of man and for the purpose of complementing man.[10] She is therefore not an end in herself, but a functionary of man's fulfillment. Man is the subject; woman is the object, the *other*. Given the pervasiveness of this world view, the American male novelist's inability to assign full humanity to his female characters is partially understandable.

The validity of some feminist critiques of American male novelists has been questioned. The charge has been made that the writers they choose for their illustrations of male deficiencies are not representative.[11] To avoid such a charge, this study will focus on three writers who have been central in the study of American literature in this century, writers whose significance is unquestioned. William Faulkner, Ernest Hemingway, and John Steinbeck are not only widely read, but their influence on American letters is telling. Yet their deficiencies in the portrayal of female characters have long been a subject of interest to feminists and nonfeminists alike. Long before Fiedler's all-inclusive condemnation of our male novelists and long before the rebirth of the women's movement in the sixties, individual critics had found fault with Faulkner, Hemingway, and Steinbeck for the inadequate realization of their female characters.

Perhaps the first critic to be sensitive to Hemingway's distorted depiction of women was Edmund Wilson. As early as 1939 Wilson discerned what he called Hemingway's growing antagonism to women, particularly evident in "The Short Happy Life of Francis Macomber" and "The Snows of Kilimanjaro" as well as *The Fifth Column*. Wilson observed that the antagonism came through in those works principally, but that the tendency could be traced through many of the other short stories such as "The Doctor and the Doctor's Wife," "Cross-Country Snow," "Hills like White Elephants," "A Canary for One," and "An Alpine Idyll."[12] In Wilson's reading, Hemingway's early women are all frustrated or thwarted or die because of their relationships with men. Only the docile, submissive, "infra-Anglo Saxon" types provide satisfactory partners, and at that they often suffer the same fate as their more aggressive sisters. Wilson reasoned that there was a marked similarity between Hemingway and Kipling in this tendency. He defined it as a split attitude toward women, which he labeled as an "instinct to get the woman down." In Hemingway this is displayed initially in the early Michigan woods stories and gradually changes in the African stories to a fear that the woman will get the man down.

Carlos Baker's rationalization for Hemingway's failure to "tell it the way it was" in his depiction of half the human race is that Hemingway sees women as aspects of the poetry of things. "His heroines, to make the statement exactly, are meant to show a symbolic or ritualistic function in the service of the artist and the service of man."[13] Therefore, since they act as functionaries, usually occupying the two extremes of destructive deadliness or devoted docility, realistic portraiture is not required. Baker's defense corroborates the claims of those who charge Hemingway with seeing woman only as *other*.

Hemingway came under attack because his females are not real, or as Fiedler put it, not there at all. "There are no women in Hemingway's books," Fiedler contends, because "in no case can he quite succeed in making his females human...."[14] Faulkner, on the other hand, has been labeled an obsessive misogynist. Fiedler states, "In no other writer in the world do pejorative stereotypes of women appear with greater frequency and on more levels...."[15] Furthermore, Fiedler contends that if Faulkner had been writing about any racial minority as he wrote about women his books would have been banned. However, since Faulkner's attitude reflects "a body of prejudice so deeply ingrained in Americans that even hysterically rendered it seems too familiar to be shocking," it is often overlooked.[16] As Fiedler notes, Hemingway has a few natural women who are redemptive, but even Faulkner's "dewiest dells" turn out to be destroyers rather than redeemers.

Maxwell Geismar identifies Faulkner's misogyny with a protest against life. He diagnoses this attitude as "a hatred of life so compelling" that the crux of Faulkner's discontent comes to rest on women as the source of life.[17] Geismar found that in Faulkner there is a definite disgust with the present which represents man's progress and a longing for the past when things were supposedly different. Long before theorists in the women's movement linked women and blacks as oppressed groups, Faulkner linked them in another way. In Geismar's view the woman, who is seen as the symbol of the southern age of chivalry which has been perverted, and the black, whose emancipation is seen as the cause of the loss of the past life, are both objects of Faulkner's enmity. [18]

More recent studies, those that have had the benefit of some biographical materials that were not made public during Faulkner's lifetime, suggest that Faulkner's misogyny is the counterpart of his idealization of women. Gail Mortimer asserts: "The other side of this powerful longing for romantic passion is an equally deep distrust and bitterness toward women." The results are female characters who are "distorted or mythicized beings, the projection of a masculine consciousness at its most vulnerable." [19]

Whereas Hemingway is criticized for his unrealistic depiction of women and Faulkner for his malevolent one, in analyzing Steinbeck's fictional female creations, one encounters the problem of quantity as well as the problem of quality. There is a scarcity of women in the majority of Steinbeck's novels. Peter Lisca points out the paucity of what might be called romantic love. Male friendships are the focus, not love. Citing the close male relationships in 11 of Steinbeck's novels, Lisca comments, "There are women in these novels, but their allurements are overshadowed by the more solid attractions of male companionship." [20] Another interesting phenomenon, pointed out by Lisca, is that in all of Steinbeck's works there are only a half dozen unmarried women who are not professional whores. "In the world of his fiction women do have a place, but they seem compelled to chose between home-making and whoredom." [21] Robert Morsberger is another who has written on the scarcity of women and abundance of prostitutes in Steinbeck's works. [22] Claude-Edmonde Magny also defines the subordinate and rather special role that women are relegated to in all of Steinbeck's novels. Instead of focusing on the traditional boy-meets-girl, the plot usually involves the encounter of two men and all that ensues from that particular relationship. This is true of Mac and Jim (*In Dubious Battle*), George and Lennie (*Of Mice and Men*), and Danny and Pilon (*Tortilla Flat*) to name a few examples. Magny questions Steinbeck's primary focus on male couples, concluding that "the most apparent meaning—and one that is contrapuntally reinforced by other themes in the novels mentioned—is the expulsion of Woman from the true human community." [23]

A reasonable argument can be made for the choice of Hemingway, Faulkner, and Steinbeck as representative American male authors. These three men come from widely varying geographical locations: the North, the South, and the West Coast. Stylistically they run the gamut from the spare to the prolix. Their range of subject matter is decidedly diverse. All three are

Nobel Prize winners and as such may be seen by the international community as representative of the best in American writing. They are widely translated and published.

The awarding of the Nobel Prize to these three writers provides a useful point of departure for a discussion of their characterization of women. The Nobel committee's criterion for the Nobel Prize for Literature is that it shall be awarded to the person whose work is the most outstanding "work of an idealistic tendency." Yet, all of the American winners of this award, with the exception of Pearl Buck, have been widely regarded as prophets of pessimism. Pearl Buck, the only American woman to win the Nobel Prize for Literature, is alone in her obvious confidence in individual importance and perception of a universal goodness innate in the particulars of existence. Walter E. Kidd, in his introduction to *American Winners of the Nobel Prize,* observes that all American winners, Pearl Buck excepted, "express the pervasive disillusion and pessimism during and between two world wars. Bitter disillusion, neurotic behavior, spiritual sterility, and physical and psychological ruthlessness of an industrialized society mark their writings."[24]

The pessimistic aspects of each of these writers have been delineated not only in the Nobel award presentation addresses, but also in the large body of criticism of their works. Faulkner's work is described by Gustaf Hellstrom, member of the Swedish Academy, in his presentation address as a work that grew out of "defeat and the consequences of defeat." Hellstom elaborates: "Faulkner has often been described as a determinist. He himself, however, has never claimed to adhere to any special philosophy of life. Briefly, his view of life may perhaps be summed up in his own words: that the whole thing (perhaps?) signifies nothing."[25] Hellstrom's speech captures the sense of nihilistic despair that a majority of readers feel when faced with the Yoknapatawphian world. A few empathetic individuals are doomed and much of the rest of Faulkner's cast of characters is composed of warped, degenerate, mentally and emotionally disturbed, spiritually impoverished creatures. In few of Faulkner's works is there even what might be called a hero, an individual, however flawed, that one would wish to identify with. The experiences of his protagonists can be so alien that they do not engage the emotions, only the intellect. Faulkner's tragedy is anguished, contorted, nonelevating, and often even his comedy is not light. It is the comedy of irony and often has a sadistic thrust, laughing at pain and stupidity, macabre jokes with humanity as their butt.

Carlos Baker, Allen Guttman and Clinton S. Burhans, Jr. are among those who have commented on the tragic implications of Hemingway's novels.[26] Philip Young describes the Hemingway world as "one in which things do not grow or bear fruit, but explode, break, decompose, or are eaten away.... It is a barren world of fragments which lies before us like a land of bad dreams, where a few pathetic idylls and partial triumphs relieve the otherwise steady diet of nightmare."[27] The fact that Hemingway viewed life as a tragedy with only one end is well documented in his letters. In his Nobel presentation address, Anders Oesterling, the permanent secretary of the Swedish Academy, concedes that "Hemingway's earlier writings displayed brutal, cynical and callous signs which may be considered at variance with the Nobel Prize requirements for a work of ideal tendencies."[28] Ibsen had been rejected by the Academy as "the bleak champion of negativity," but Hemingway "the author of *Nada*" was honored.

Eight years later, in his presentation address to John Steinbeck, Oesterling noted the dark tenor of Steinbeck's "grim humor." Even his comic novel *Cannery Row* had been called a "poisonous creampuff" by one critic. Oesterling cites Steinbeck's "often cruel and crude motif." The characters who populate Steinbeck's world have been variously pictured as the oppressed, the distressed, the misfits, the subrational, and the inarticulate. Kidd states that the animal level of these characters reveals the "disintegration, vulgarity, and other evils of society."[29] Steinbeck's "nonteleological" or "is-thinking" approach connotes a strong degree of moral fatalism. Freeman Champney explains the effect of this approach on the message of the novels: "When he abandons Man as Man for Man as Biological Freak he goes all the way. He jettisons not only hope and progress but cause and effect as well."[30]

Notwithstanding the dismal world pictures presented in the works of these three men, the Academy found enough of an affirmative nature in them to justify the awards. Faulkner's acceptance speech seemed to substantiate their decision. Its optimistic message produced a torrent of postprize criticism reevaluating what had hitherto been perceived as pessimistic work. The speech, quoted ad nauseam, has become the jumping-off place for much of what has been written about Faulkner since 1949. In it Faulkner utters his avowal of man's worth. He sounds a prophecy that man will not only endure, but prevail. Though the fact that man will prevail is the climax of the speech, the keynote of Faulkner's message is in man's ability to endure.[31]

Endurance is also a key quality in Hemingway's philosophy. Primarily this is endurance of a spiritual nature. Santiago, the hero of the book that is cited as the occasion for the Nobel award, states it succinctly: "Man was not made for defeat. A man can be destroyed, but not defeated" (OMAS, 103). Steinbeck's acceptance speech also echoes attitudes expressed by Faulkner and Hemingway. In it he cites "humanity's long proud history of standing firm against natural enemies, sometimes in the face of almost certain defeat and extinctions...."[32]

There would seem to be major obstacles to correlating the affirmations of these authors with the events portrayed in their works, which for the most part are discouraging and disheartening. It is in the characterizations of their women, though, that the possibility of such a reconciliation presents itself. Amidst their generally negative portraitures of humanity and modern society, all three authors create a few characters who symbolize or represent the positive possibilities for human survival. Most of these enduring characters reflect aspects of the basic primitivism that links the works of Faulkner, Hemingway, and Steinbeck.[33] A pervasive disillusionment with contemporary life and its neuroses caused these three writers to see in those characters who have been least affected by the influences of society, who have remained closest to nature, who have been the least "civilized," the primary hope for human survival. Because "primitives" have been the least affected by the ills of modern life, they are the best equipped to endure it. Woman, since she is generally regarded as *other*, more akin to nature and less "civilized" than man, is included with the Negro, the Indian, the peasant, and other enduring primitives in their works.[34] As different as the works of these three writers are, there is one character type that appears with significant consistency in many of their works. This character, who represents hope for human survival and belief in the human capacity for endurance, I have chosen to call "the indestructible woman."[35]

The indestructible woman, present in various manifestations but with marked regularity in the works of Faulkner, Hemingway, and Steinbeck, is a product not only of their basic primitivism, but also of their initial desire to present their material objectively, a methodology which corresponds in some ways to the naturalistic approach to literature. Because of their general distrust of the word, all three attempted, early in their careers, to create an objective and impersonal literature.[36] Their works often emphasize an amoral view of the struggle in which the human animal finds itself; they are generally pessimistic in their view of human capabilities and try to present frank and almost clinically accurate portrayals of the human being as an animal driven by fundamental urges, the victim of biological and socioeconomic forces beyond control and understanding. In an admittedly oversimplified sense, their ersatz naturalism parallels in fiction the principles of scientific determinism. Consciously or unconsciously, their indestructible female derives in part from the physicist's concept of matter, which, according to the scientific myth, can change form, but can never be destroyed.

The correlation of woman with matter is easily accomplished imaginatively. Instances of this are legion. In the words of Nietzsche, "Inorganic matter is the maternal bosom." The very names for the maternal parent, mater-materies-matrix, mean matter. In most cultures' creation myths, the Earth is female, Mother Earth. Mother Earth and Mother Nature are two very nearly universal personifications of the Eternal Woman. Woman is matter and Man is spirit in the archetypal symbolism of things. "While the masculine mysteries start from the priority of the spirit and look upon the reality of the phenomenal world and of matter as the creation of spirit, the feminine mysteries start from the priority of the phenomenal 'material' world, from which the spiritual is born."[37]

Both fear and awe characterize the reaction to the phenomenon of the mystery of matter. This reaction has resulted in both pejorative and simplistic depictions of women in literature, often products of the male writer's inability to come to terms with the *otherness* of woman. It is apparent in the traditional canon of American literature. It is apparent in the works of Faulkner, Hemingway, and Steinbeck. The result is a paradoxical characterization which has drawn criticisms for its deficiencies and yet produced an affirmative type, the indestructible woman, who, like Mother Nature, is sometimes cruel and sometimes kind but always enduring. The indestructible woman is an ambivalent character; she is at once sustaining and suffocating. Like Mother Earth she gives life; like Mother Earth she devours the bones of her children. Not only earth, but the various manifestations of nature are envisioned as female: oceans and mountains are female in their endurance—and in their deadliness. Man attempts to conquer them as he does nature. Though he may be momentarily successful, eventually he is engulfed by the maternal oneness.

Psychologically, the twin reactions of attraction and repulsion are part of each man's impulse toward individuation. "Perhaps man's greatest need was to separate himself from the feminine, the maternal oneness. In order to create himself he had to discriminate the masculine from the feminine, *to discriminate against the feminine*, knowing its formlessness to be his greatest enemy."[38] Thus woman, who is symbolically matter, which has to be tamed, restructured, and used to the purposes of the spirit, yet retains a mysterious quality that, like matter in its indestructibility, defies ultimate subjugation to the uses of man. Faulkner, Hemingway, and Steinbeck's indestructible women characters are, in part, products of the contradictory psychological reactions which result from each man's need to differentiate himself from the earth, the body, the formlessness that woman represents, while still retaining a respect for the primacy of matter. This may account for what many critics see as the lack of humanity in their female characters, for when woman becomes the symbol for the earth and the body, she loses her individual humanity. "To be earth and body is not personal, it is deeper than personal."[39] Though these authors have thus deprived woman of her full humanity in the temporal scene of contemporary society, they have assigned her a significant role in the greater drama of the survival of the species.

2

Faulkner

Faulkner's conscious and unconscious utilization of universal and regional myths and archetypes has been well established by both literary criticism and biographical studies. Though he was a very private person in the early period of his career, in later years, particularly during his stay as writer-in-residence at the University of Virginia, Faulkner openly discussed his work and answered questions about it. His comments provide important clues about the special role woman plays in his literary schema.

A large portion of Faulkner criticism proceeds from archetypal, mythic, and/or psychological premises, premises which Faulkner validated by the comments he made about his conscious techniques and their possible underlying unconscious motivations. When responding to questions about his plots and characters, he made it quite clear that though he did not "have time to be conscious of all the symbolism," since his primary task was to create "flesh-and-blood human beings," much unconscious symbolism was possible.[1] When questioned about correspondences between his works and biblical and mythic situations, he denied deliberate duplication while acceding to the possibility that unconscious correspondences were probable.[2] Frequently, Faukner's response to variant interpretations of his works was, "That's possible. Of course I didn't think of that at the time... but that's possible, that's valid."[3] Faulkner contended that a writer borrowed from everything in his experience and therefore the possibility of unconscious duplications was highly probable.

Tracking the sources of these unconscious duplications has been the business of many astute Faulkner scholars. Joseph Blotner has catalogued Faulkner's library.[4] David Minter evaluated the influences of his reading, particularly in nineteenth-century literature.[5] Others have explored Faulkner's use of contemporary psychological and scientific works.[6] Among Faulkner's favorite authors were Shakespeare, Balzac, Flaubert, Dickens, Melville, Twain, Conrad, and Joyce. When he liked a book, he went back to it repeatedly.[7] He was well read in the King James Version of the Bible and in classical mythology as well as in the works of the classical anthropologists such as Sir James Frazer, Jane Harrison, and Gilbert Murray. Faulkner's own words are a good indication of how he used these sources. He defined an author's memory as "a little of kleptomania" adding, "He misses very little and when the need comes he digs out things that he didn't know where he saw— which to him don't matter, he may have stolen it—he probably did—but to him that's not important. The important thing is if he use it worthily."[8] Furthermore, Faulkner verified the fact that he had a good memory: "I doubt if I've forgotten anything I ever read."[9]

Faulkner, not only drew on what he read, but also had a keen ear. His excellent transcription of the various Southern dialects attests to that. His sources also included the oral tradition of Mississippi. As Richard P. Adams explains it:

> In addition, he was saturated with talk, which is still an artistic medium in north Mississippi, and from which, as he said in an interview or two, he got much of his awareness of the traditions, legends, and what we may call mythology of the South. He used this material in the same way as he used the Bible and the classical mythology, as a thief by sovereign right, and often with scant respect for the pieties in which it might be invested by conventional people.[10]

Faulkner's indestructible women were developed in just such a manner. They derived from the conscious and subconscious use of the various mythologies, both regional and universal, that permeated Faulkner's creative processes. His indestructible woman is a composite, created in a uniquely Faulknerian style. Her genesis is classical, her education southern colloquial, and her specifics uniquely Yoknapatawphian, designed with scant respect for conventional pieties.

Thadious Davis, in *Faulkner's "Negro,"* develops a thesis about the "artistic" burden Faulkner places on his "Negro." Davis explains that while Negroes in the South served as a metaphor for change, they were seen also as the lone constants in a world of flux.[11] Faulkner's indestructible women serve an analogous function. Theirs is the artistic burden of being the symbols for endurance in a world of constant change. Faulkner's male characters are often beings who are literally and figuratively divided. Characters such as Darl Bundren even seem able to be in two places at one time, while others such as Joe Christmas and Popeye are psychologically rent in two. Quentin Compson is torn, among other things, between his criticism of and love for the South. Faulkner's women, however, maintain a centeredness the men lack. They instinctively know their roles in the eternal scheme of things. Temporarily, Faulkner may allow such female characters as Temple Drake, Drusilla Hawk, and Linda Snopes to rebel against the traditional constraints of femininity, but their rebellion is short-lived. In the context of the eternal verities, these women inevitably assume their roles as constants: the perpetuators of tradition, the providers of continuity. The literature that Faulkner wrote is often complicated, obfuscated, and perplexing; his indestructible women characters are no less so.

While women make up a small proportion of the characters in the works of Hemingway and Steinbeck, there are women in abundance in Faulkner's works. His interest in them and awe of them was repeatedly articulated. When asked which he preferred to write about, men or women, he replied, "It's much more fun to try to write about women because I think women are marvelous, they're wonderful, and I know very little about them, and so I just—it's much more fun to try to write about women than about men—more difficult, yes."[12] In the same vein he spoke of the inspiration for writing his novel *Light in August*: "It was—that was out of my admiration for women, for the courage and endurance of women."[13] The woman he refers to in that novel is, of course, Lena Grove, a prime example of the indestructible woman.

Faulkner's expression of this attitude toward women was communicated in his fiction through characterization, theme, and plot pattern. Faulkner's female characters are often described, either by the omniscient narrator or some other character, in terms that suggest their oneness with the Eternal Feminine, particularly in her manifestation as Earth Goddess. This is significant in the communication of her indestructibility because, in that prenuclear period in which Faulkner wrote, it was presumed that though one generation would succeed another, the earth would abide. Women, then, either in their manifestation as earth goddesses or because of their special affinity with the Earth, their mother, partake of the earth's enduring nature.

A number of Faulkner's indestructible women are developed using imagery that stresses their close identification with the earth. Lena Grove in *Light in August* is described in terms that suggest her oneness with nature. The sylvan imagery invoked by her name provides the initial clue. Her description compounds the connection. She is depicted as one who "sits quite still, hearing and feeling the implacable and immemorial earth, but without fear or alarm"(LIA, 25). Her interconnectedness with the earth is emphasized by Faulkner when he describes the manner of her movements. When she walks, the ground that she traverses is described as "the old earth *of* and *with* and *by* which she lives" (LIA, 23; emphasis mine).

Her connection to mythological woman was corroborated by Faulkner in his discussion of the title, *Light in August*. He explained that the light in the title was "of a luminosity older than our Christian civilization." Relating this to Lena he elaborated:

> Maybe the connection was with Lena Grove, who had something of that pagan quality of being able to assume everything. . . . But as far as she was concerned, she didn't especially

need any father for it [her expected child], any more than the women that—on whom Jupiter begot children were anxious for a home and a father. It was enough to have had the child. And that was all that meant, just that luminous lambent quality of an older light than ours.[14]

Obviously, Lena is seen by her creator as being of a species whose connections go beyond the temporal and whose needs and values are not those of ordinary humans. In Faulkner's description, Lena becomes more than human. While on one level she is an ignorant country girl, exploring a bit before she settles down, she is also a mythological demi-goddess, serenely seeing to the earth's repopulation.

Her fertility and her connection to earth are a combination that occurs with some frequency in Faulkner's indestructible women. An adjective Faulkner uses repeatedly to describe the earth is "fecund." He also uses that adjective in connection with females and Negroes, a linguistic linkage that corroborates the underlying primitivistic attitude that saw both Negroes and women as enduring because of their affinity to the earth. In one passage, the "savage and fecund odor of the earth" is described (LIA, 356); when Joe Christmas is in Freedman Town the use of the word again connects women, blacks, and earth: "On all sides, even within him, the bodiless fecundmellow voices of Negro women murmured. It was as though he and all other manshaped life about him had been returned to the lightless hot wet primogenitive Female" (LIA, 100). In this passage, the call of women's voices is a call to the primitive state. More than that, the imagery strongly suggests a return to the womb which could also be the earth. Generation is female.

While the previous attitude cannot necessarily be attributed to Faulkner, since it is Joe Christmas whose thoughts are being presented, it is significant that Hightower, whose sensibility should be quite different from Christmas's, expresses similar thoughts. Hightower muses after the delivery of Lena's baby and in his musing connects the land, the woman, and the black with luck and fertility. To him, Lena's baby is luck returned to the land. With its birth, he feels the return of "rich fields, and of the rich fecund black life of the quarters, the mellow shouts, the presence of fecund women, the prolific naked children..." (LIA, 357). When such similar imagery is evoked by such disparate points of view as those of the omniscient narrator, Joe Christmas, and Gail Hightower, there is a strong implication that these connections arose from Faulkner's perception.

Lena Grove is but one of the women in Faulkner's works who embodies the correlation of woman and nature. The women in *Sanctuary* are also described in terms of their leguminous qualities. Narcissa Benbow is "living a life of serene vegetation like perpetual corn or wheat," and Horace's stepdaughter Little Belle is connected with vineyards and arbors. Horace, thinking of her, describes "the delicate and urgent mammalian whisper of that curious small flesh ... in which appeared to be vatted delicately some seething sympathy with the blossoming grape" (S, 200). He describes her voice as being like "the murmer of the wild grape itself" (S, 13). When he looks at her picture the smell of honeysuckle pervades his senses.

While Narcissa and Little Belle are described in terms of bounteous nature, Faulkner's sense of the ironic macabre is evidenced in the imagery that connects Temple Drake with the dried up or discarded fruits of nature. Temple, as nature perverted, is associated with the shucks rather than the ripe ears of corn. She is bedded on a cornshuck mattress, she takes refuge in a bin of cottonseed hulls and dried corncobs, and finally she is raped with a dry corncob rather than a living penis. All possibility of fecundity is eliminated. Even her name is a perverted nature image, the drake being the male rather than the female duck. Though she is associated with nature images, it is with dry and sterile nature.

Ruby Godwin is not described in vegetative adjectives or images, but her omnipresent baby is a vivid reminder of her maternal and therefore productive capacities. The baby is with her at the Frenchman's place when she is acting as cook, the nourisher as well as the maternal; it is with her at the spring when she tries to get away. It is even in her arms at such incongruous moments as when she is being slapped by Godwin or when she offers herself to Horace in exchange for his help, a scene which depicts her in the roles of woman as mother and sex object in one. Whether she be servant, wife, woman, or whore, she is always the eternal mother, baby on hip, instinctually guarding and protecting the next generation.

Twice in the novel Horace makes the observation that nature is female, thus underlining the identification of woman with Mother Nature or the Earth Goddess. On one occasion he says, "That's why we know that nature is a she; because of that conspiracy between female flesh and female season" (S, 11). At another point Horace speaks words that could be the articulation of Faulkner's primitivism when he says, "That's why nature is 'she' and Progress is 'he'; nature made the grape arbor, but Progress invented the mirror." The mirror in this situation is the symbol for the revelation of Little Belle's dissimulation. The mirror is used for deception; the grape arbor sustains and provides.

In *The Sound and the Fury* it is the cynical Mr. Compson who voices the connection between women and nature. He tries to explain to Quentin that the loss of Caddy's virginity is inevitable. "Father said 'Women are never virgins. Purity is a negative state and therefore contrary to nature'" (SF, 135). Caddy's sexuality is not contrary to nature. It is the rigidity, the "unnatural" standards of the Compson family that drive Caddy away and deprive the family of her loving and giving character. Caddy is a natural woman, responding to her sexual urges, doing her part in the procreation of the species. When the

Compson inability to accept Caddy's actions drives her away, the family is left in the hands of two "unnatural" characters, Mrs. Compson and Jason. Mrs. Compson is the antithesis of a "natural" mother for she cannot or does not love her children; Jason is the "unnatural" man, one who does not propagate. In the hands of these unnatural creatures, the line would die out. Only through Caddy and then her daughter can nature assure the continuation of the line.

Whereas Mr. Compson's connection of women and nature is a philosophical one, Benjy must rely on his sense of smell to fuse Caddy with nature. For Benjy, Caddy's natural smell is like leaves and trees. His reactions are not complicated; his perception of her connection to nature is straightforward. "Caddy knelt and put her arms around me and her cold bright face against mine. She smelled like trees" (SF, 28). The tree motif is an interesting one. Sally R. Page suggests that "Since Caddy is primarily 'mother' to Benjy, it is probable that the 'tree' motif in *The Sound and the Fury* is meant to suggest that Caddy is a 'mother of life' figure."[15] Walter Brylowski notes Faulkner's connection of trees with virginal girls, not with mother figures. Such a connection would be more in keeping with a number of traditional myths in which chaste young nymphs are turned into trees, or flowers, or springs rather than be seduced by some lustful god, such as the story of the independent, love-and-marriage hating young huntress Daphne, who turns into a laurel rather than submit to Apollo. In *The Sound and the Fury* Caddy is associated with tree smells as long as she is virginal. When she puts on perfume to attract the boys, when she is in the swing with Charlie, and when she has had her first complete sexual experience, Benjy immediately notices the difference in her smell. She no longer smells like trees.

The tree as a symbol for Caddy is reinforced by the fact that the two dominant images of the novel have to do with trees. Faulkner stated that the book "began with the picture of the little girl's muddy drawers, climbing that tree to look in the parlor window with her brothers that didn't have the courage to climb the tree waiting to see what she saw."[16] In most of the critical discussion which is part of what Eric Sundquist calls "The Myth of *The Sound and the Fury*," attention has been focused on the muddy drawers, which are very important, but to the exclusion of the tree.[17] The tree, however, is a crucial component of this image. In that scene, which Faulkner saw as his impetus for writing the book, the tree serves as Caddy's passageway to an encounter with the realities of existence, one of which is death. Caddy is courageous enough to accept this reality as well as its opposite, which is her sexuality. A tree (the cedar) is also associated with her first explorations of the male/female relationship. In that situation, and quite appropriately, the smell of honeysuckle is intermingled with the smell of trees. In his imagery Faulkner is moving from the chaste connections of tree symbolism to the erotic connotations of flower symbolism. Quentin's perceptions of Caddy are infused with flower and tree smells. In his attempt to substitute himself for Caddy's male companions he says, "It was me you thought I was in the house where that damn honey suckle trying not to think the swing the cedars the secret surges the breathing locked drinking the wild breath tHE YES YES YES YES" (SF, 167).

Another important tree that is used as a passage to experience is the tree that Caddy's daughter, Quentin II, uses to escape from Jason.[18] The tree is also Quentin II's vehicle for the fulfillment of her sexuality as it is used for all her rendezvous. When Luster is asked about her beaux, he replies, "They comes every night she can climb down that tree" (SF, 69). Significantly, the tree that Quentin II uses for her escape from the Compsons is a blossoming pear tree: "The window was open. A pear tree grew there, close against the house. It was in bloom and the branches scraped and rasped against the house and the myriad air, driving in the window, brought into the room the forlorn scent of the blossoms" (SF, 298). The suggestion of fruitfulness is implicit and the scent of the blossoms suggests Quentin II's sexuality. The tree also suggests continuity and female cycles as it is quite possibly the same pear tree Caddy, her mother, used to witness the death of her grandmother.

Besides the tree imagery that is associated with Caddy, both Quentin and Benjy also relate her to water. The association of woman with water is an ancient one and basic in female symbology. Another characteristic of this same symbology is the identification of woman as vessel. She is the vessel man goes "into," the vessel for carrying and bringing forth the child, the vessel for milk to feed the child. The natural elements that are essentially connected with vessel symbolism include both earth and water. The water is of various types: one is the containing water which is the primordial womb of life from which in innumerable myths life is born. But the waters of the female are not only the maternal waters that contain (amniotic fluid), but also the waters of nourishment (milk), since all living things build up or preserve their existence with the water or milk of the earth. Thus water can be symbolically related to the breast as well as the womb and the rain and the earth waters (springs, lakes, ponds) are as the milk of the earth body.[19] The association of woman with milk-producing animals, especially the cow, is one that Faulkner uses frequently. As Lederer explains: "In the mythological apperception of early man, breast and milk and rain; and woman and cow and earth and spring and stream belong together: the ground water belonged to the belly–womb region, the heavenly rain to the breast region of the Feminine."[20] Faulkner uses these connections when he describes Dilsey, who is surrogate mother and nourisher of the Compson family. He says that she "stood like a cow in the rain" (SF, 288).

But to return to the association of Caddy with water, just the suggestion of water is enough to make Benjy's mind immediately travel to memories of

Caddy splashing in the branch. After much splashing and playing, and Caddy teasing with threats to run away, she reassures Benjy that she will not. Caddy in this role, both virginal and nurturant, smells a special way to Benjy: "Caddy smelled like trees in the rain" (SF, 38).

Quentin's association of Caddy with water is more complex. One of Quentin's problems is that he feels that he has had no mother. Mrs. Compson has abdicated her maternal role. He is very conscious of this loss. "If I could say Mother. Mother" (SF, 114), and "if I'd just had a mother so I could say Mother Mother" (SF, 190) are his cries. Since he has been rejected by his mother, he fastens his needs onto the person of his sister, who attempts to be surrogate mother to all the boys because "Mother's sick. She and Damuddy are both sick" (SF, 93). Mother's "sickness" is passed on to the family and Quentin must attempt a "sick" method of replacing his mother. His desire to isolate his sister from the natural processes of life takes the form of an invented incest. He does not want to mature and he does not want her to. He wants to regress, in effect, to return to the womb. By his suicide he does just that; he returns to the water. Jung has described the desire for drowning as a desire to be reabsorbed into the mother, a death which is "a deep personal longing for quiet and for the profound peace of non-existence, for dreamless sleep in the ebb and flow of the sea of life."[21] By the act of drowning himself, Quentin can metaphorically have both the mother he never had and the sister he wanted.

In his development of the theme of woman's indestructibility, Faulkner connects woman with the earth, with fertility, and with such living organisms as animals, flowers, and trees, to emphasize woman's oneness with nature. Water imagery is another of his methods of suggesting woman's connection with the primordial womb and the flow of life. Woman's connection with nature and natural cycles is also emphasized by Faulkner's use of moon imagery in developing his female characters. The triune goddess or Hecate Triformis is a conventional female goddess, who is, among other things, the moon goddess and symbolically woman has been represented by the moon. "The moon, first as an influence on fertility and later as a deity, has been considered throughout the ages to be in peculiar relation to women."[22] The moon has a cyclic or changing character, just as woman does, and these cycles can be compared to the three stages of a woman's life. Various of Faulkner's works develop the theme of woman's singular relationship with the moon. In his development of the indestructible woman, he often utilizes the pattern of tripartite woman: maid, mother, and crone.

Specific connections between women and the moon are articulated by Mr. Compson in *The Sound and the Fury*. Quentin recalls his father's trying to explain the lunar periodicity of the menstrual cycle: "Because women so delicate so mysterious Father said. Delicate equilibrium of periodic filth between two moons balanced. Moons he said full and yellow as harvest moons her hip thighs..." (SF, 147). The image of periodic filth between two moons that are also the female pelvis is a repetition of the image of Caddy's muddy drawers as she climbs the pear tree in the moonlight, an image which is reinforced by "the soiled undergarment of cheap silk" that Quentin II leaves behind on the floor of her room. In each case the image connects earth, filth, mud, or soil with moonlight as a simulacrum of the nature and character of the female.

Not only through his utilization of nature imagery, with its focus on the "earthiness" of feminine character, to develop his indestructible women, but also in statements he made about women, Faulkner emphasizes the grounded nature of women's character. In a nostalgic essay, "Mississippi," Faulkner explains that he liked to think that his mother and Caroline Barr, his "mammy," would reminisce about the days when they had a houseful of men to take care of, but he allows that "they probably didn't since women, unlike men, have learned how to live, uncomplicated by that sort of sentimentality."[23] His characterization of women both in his works and in his statements about them is couched in language that suggests their centeredness, their practicality, their strength.

His attitude toward feminine fortitude was proclaimed uncategorically: "Oh, I think that women are much stronger, much more determined than men."[24] The language he uses is telling. He speaks of women as a class, not of individual women. He speaks in generalizations about the entire gender, a linguistic structure which suggests stereotypical thinking. It bespeaks not only the notion of woman as *other*, a being of different essential nature than man, but it also suggests the southern male adulation of his women, the mothers, wives, and daughters whose safety and security were the clarion call for Confederate male derring-do, bluster, as well as for racist oppression.

Faulkner often spoke of the women of the South as the unvanquished. He told of his "undefeated spinster aunts" who were the repositories of the tales of past southern glory. The men had been defeated, he said, but the aunts, the women, had never given up the war.[25] The image of the delicate southern belle with a spine of steel is a prevalent one in southern mythology.[26] In the post-Civil War South, southern womanhood became an ideal, a symbol, a banner that was evoked to encourage and rally the men. Faulkner's consciousness of this is demonstrated in his fiction. In the short story "Dry September" woman is used as just such an icon. The plot is set in motion when McLendon musters the men in the barber shop to his cause—lynching Willie Mays—by rallying them round the banner of the purity of southern womanhood. He does not refer specifically to Miss Minnie Cooper, the woman whose virtue was supposedly assaulted. Her virtue, as we learn later in the story, has been questionable since her affair with the teller some years earlier. The term he uses is "a white woman," the inference being that the individual woman is not significant but the class is. The drummer in the barber's chair responds in kind; he says, "I don't live here, but by God, if our mothers and wives and sisters—" never concluding a sentence that did not need finishing in that context.

Virtue, character, and individual circumstance are irrelevant when woman loses her human identity and becomes an object of reverence. In this situation the distance between the sexes is widened. As the venerated object, woman is put on a pedestal, and pedestals are a special kind of prison. Those on them may be held in awe, but they are also kept apart from the human community. This distance lends them a mystery; and mysteries are paradoxical. They both attract and repel, qualities that are obvious in Faulkner's characterization of the attitudes of such diverse characters as Joe Christmas, Gavin Stevens, and Horace Benbow toward the various women in their lives.

In "Dry September" as well as in many of his other works, Faulkner illustrates his awareness of how the myth of southern woman operated in his society to the detriment of both women and blacks. A number of his stories are obvious debunkings of the myth. Still, as Meta Carpenter Wilde and other biographers have pointed out, Faulkner's manner toward women was ever that of the southern gentleman. The ambivalences present in many of Faulkner's female characterizations are illustrative of the tensions that existed between what Faulkner knew as a writer and the emotional residue of his upbringing.[27]

The southern lady's impregnable purity is a particularly troubling aspect of the myth of southern womanhood and Faulkner was one of its chief debunkers. Before and after the Civil War, the mythic purity of southern womanhood was used by white males as the rationale for many of their sexual and violent excesses against both black women and men. Since the white woman was seen as a pure and therefore nonsexual being, white men rationalized their sexual use of black women as a safety valve to release the tensions of their grosser natures. Blacks were seen as more animalistic and therefore less sexually restrained beings. As white men were forcing their sexual attentions on black women, they feared a reciprocal desire on the part of black men. The slightest pretext was used by white men to justify the murder and castration of black men for supposed violations of southern women's purity. White men were therefore allowed access to women of both races, but black men and white women were kept in their place. Racism and sexism developed as two sides of the same coin.[28] They worked together in the South; they work together in Faulkner's development of enduring characters. The connection is an ironic one, however, because what is at work is what appears to be a kind of reverse racism and sexism. While still seeing blacks and women as inferior in the context of contemporary civilization, the paradox at work in Faulkner's fiction is that it is their very inferiority or lack of civilization that sets them apart and insures their perseverance.

Thadious Davis explains in her introduction to *Faulkner's "Negro"* that the Negro she is concerned with is an artistic conception, "the Negro" as a white man's own creation, something that has little to do with black Americans in a contemporary context. Davis explains that Faulkner's Negro lived in a world that was divided into two parts: black and white;[29] the Negro world then provided Faulkner with a useful antithesis or counterpoint to the white world. But in the southern world similarly rigid demarcations existed between the world of woman and the world of man. "Woman" in Faulkner is also man's own creation, the inhabitant of a separate world, closer to nature and uncomplicated by intellectualizing. In Faulkner's works women respond to the call of their own organs and the murmurings of nature; men hypothesize, theorize, and rationalize. Women operate by a set of values that transcends the temporal. As Colonel Sartoris explains in *The Unvanquished,* "Women cannot believe anything can be right or wrong or even very important that can be decided by a lot of little scraps of scribbled paper dropped into a box" (U, 235). Unlike the white male, who can only cross the color line as a child, white women operate comfortably in both worlds. Clytie and Judith can behave as sisters, related by their "indomitable woman blood" (A,A!, 153). Miss Habersham comes to the aid of Lucas, partially out of her sister-feeling for Molly.

Black and woman are also combined in the myth-stereotype of the mammy. Nancy Tischler describes the Negro mammy as witch, witch doctor, priest, intercessor, wet nurse, comforter, and permissive earth mother.[30] As a composite of both woman and Negro, she is doubly docile, comforting, and nurturing. Because she is black, she is stereotyped as less intelligent, more natural and childlike, and more affectionate and instinctual, an unthreatening mother figure. She is the dark, the mysterious, and the fecund personified. Her breast milk is abundant enough to feed not only her own, but also the white woman's children. Her lap is ample as sanctuary for all. She is the real mother figure in the memory of many of the southern men of Faulkner's generation. Faulkner's own mammy was so enduring that she lived to be a hundred years old. His devotion to her was such that he dedicated one of his books to her.[31]

The association of primitive sexuality with both women and Negroes is present in *The Sound and the Fury* as well as in *Light in August.* Quentin connects Caddy's sexual habits with dark woods, ditches, and pastures. Interestingly enough, most of the natural or indestructible females in Faulkner who have not kept to their chaste and cold marble pedestals give in to their natural appetites in the out-of-doors. Lena Grove climbs out a window to meet Lucas Burch; Caddy and Quentin II both climb out of windows to meet their beaux; Eula Varner and Hoake McCarron mate in the middle of a road in a thicket by a creek bridge; Dewey Dell and Addie Bundren also choose the woods for their illicit relationships. This lends to the relationships a more natural or primitive flavor; it is also more animalistic. Quentin makes the connection between race and sexuality when he asks Caddy, "Why dont you bring him to the house, Caddy? Why must you do like nigger women do in the pasture the ditches the dark woods hot hidden furious in the dark woods" (SF, 111). Though he is Quentin's psychological opposite, Jason uses similar terms to describe Caddy's daughter Quentin's sexual behavior. Jason accuses her of "going on like a nigger wench" (SF, 207). He threatens her: "When people act like niggers, no matter who they are the only thing to do is treat them like a nigger" (SF, 199).

The most blatant cultural stereotyping is at work here. Especially strong in the South, though also prevalent in the rest of the country, is the myth of Negro sexual virility and appetite. Even the most unprejudiced person learns through jokes, anecdotes, through mores and folklore, that Negroes are oversexed. "Negroes exist in a savage state of promiscuity," according to the stereotype.[32] Not only that, but they are more free in instinctual gratification, more emotional, primitive, and childlike. Concurrently, sexual stereotyping sees women as irresponsible, inconsistent, emotionally unstable, and lacking in strong superegos. In sexist imagery woman has been depicted as a mindless vessel, an emptyheaded plaything. Historically in this country the black woman has been used as exactly that: considered less than human, she has been a breeding animal to enlarge the supply of slaves and a repository for the white man's lust. Whereas the white woman could be a treasured vessel, a sometimes revered vessel, the black woman was merely a piece of property to be used, abused, and discarded, a worthless vessel. Ironically, she has then been damned for her enforced "usability." The character Nancy, who appears in various of Faulkner's stories and novels, is one of his illustrations of such abuse. In "That Evening Sun" Faulkner shows how she is used as a whore and then literally kicked in the teeth and cursed by the same man who uses her and then refuses to pay.

"Mongrelization" is a word used by racists to conjure up the horrors of integration. Properly applied the word refers to dogs and other animals, and this is precisely the image the racist has of Negro women. They are found sexually attractive and repugnant, but not in terms of human females, but as she-dogs.[33] Faulkner's characters use similar imagery to describe natural women. Both Caddy and Quentin II are called "bitches" by Jason; their canine qualities are emphasized in their descriptions. Quentin II is described as having "eyes hard as a fice dog's" (SF, 205). Caddy's face is described in terms that suggest a cur baring its teeth. When she gets angry, her upper lip begins to jump. "Everytime it jumped it would leave a little more of her teeth showing, and all the time she'd be as still as a post, not a muscle moving except her lip jerking higher and higher up her teeth" (SF, 206). Like the Negro of the myth, Caddy and Quentin II respond openly and hungrily to their natural urges, a response neither Jason nor Quentin can affect. Their carnal qualities differentiate them from the white males.

Many of Faulkner's indestructible females follow in the same pattern as the mythical Negro woman, who according to the myth of Negro sexhood "is endowed with irresistible sexual attraction and enjoys the sex act more than any creature on earth."[34] Temple Drake is pictured, after being raped, as sexually insatiable. She leans her thighs against Popeye's shoulder, caressing his arm with her flanks, rubbing against him and pleading, "Give it to me. Daddy. Daddy. Give it to me, Daddy" (S, 229). A few minutes later with Red, she writhes her loins against him, making a whimpering sound (S, 232). Her description of her sexual state as she begs Red to have intercourse with her are a direct reference to "heat," like a dog in the estrus cycle. She says, "Please. Please. Please. Dont make me wait. I'm burning up. I'm on fire, I tell you" (S, 233). In *The Sound and the Fury* Caddy's description of her reaction to her sexual relationships shows her passionate nature. Quentin asks her, "Did you love them Caddy did you love them" and her answer is, "When they touched me I died" (SF, 168). Quentin tries to believe that Caddy was forced, especially by Dalton Ames, her first sexual partner, but Caddy's answer to his questions of "do you love him" and then "you hate him dont you" is to take Quentin's hand and press it against her chest where her heart is thudding and then against her throat where her heart is hammering in her throat (SF, 169). When Quentin says the name Dalton Ames, he can feel Caddy's blood react; "her blood surged steadily beating and beating against my hand" (SF, 182). The image of Caddy is that of a woman at the mercy of her physical urges.

The irresistible sexual attraction and heat of Eula Varner's sexuality is described when Manfred De Spain first sees her, "walking in the Square giving off that terrifying impression that in another second her flesh itself would burn her garments off" (T, 14). She expresses her lack of control of her passions when she tells Gavin Stevens, "Don't expect. You just are, and you need, and you must, and so you do. That's all" (T, 94). These women's lack of control of their sexuality may be individually destructive, but in the long run it is beneficial for humankind. Nature insures, as she does through the canine estrus cycle, the perpetuation of the species.

Addie Bundren in *As I Lay Dying* is one of Faulkner's most complex natural women. Her identification with the earth and her passionate nature are made evident in several passages of monologue as well as in descriptions of her. Primitive that she is, she escapes from the things of man, i. e., institutions, and instead of going to a manmade retreat, home, she goes to a spring. "It would be quiet there then, with the water bubbling up and away and the sun slanting quiet in the trees and the quiet smelling of damp and rotting leaves and new earth; especially in the early spring, for it was worst then" (AILD, 161). This passage illustrates how Addie's drives and moods are allied to the changing seasons; it also juxtaposes images of death and decay with images of rebirth, a combination which will be examined further in the discussion of Faulkner's use of the Demeter/Persephone myth. Addie's basic, primitive, and natural instincts are also stressed in another passage where she identifies with the wild geese going north.

Once Addie has responded to the mating urges of her flesh, because there is no other plausible explanation given for her marrying Anse beyond the desire to escape her frustration, and once she realizes that just the physical act itself is not enough to fulfill her need, she returns to an identification with the voice of the land. She lies in bed with Anse, who is now figuratively dead to her, and she hears the land that is part of her blood and flesh (AILD, 165). Addie identifies so completely with the land that she feels that her actions are responses to its blood and voice. Her reason for living she defines as "the duty to the alive, to the terrible blood and the red bitter flood boiling throughout the land" (AILD, 166). The obvious connection between Addie and the land is strengthened as she describes the blood, particularly the "red bitter flood," which is analagous to the menstrual flow. She is then saying that she must live in order to perform her duty to "the alive," the species, through its perpetuation which is insured by her fertility. When she lies in bed with Anse, though she refuses him, she hears "the dark land talking the voiceless speech." The location for her mating with Whitfield is in the woods rather than in a room. When she has children, she feels that they are of her alone. The attitude that she expresses is one that underlines her role as an Earth Goddess. She is not unlike the incarnations of the goddess who reigned as queens in Eleusis. Kings were supplied yearly; they were interchangeable and dispensable. The fertility of the earth is the goal. In the Eleusinian context there is only the Earth Mother. We are all the children of the earth, our Mother; no father is mentioned. The fatherland is the state, the government, abstractions conceived by the mind of men. As Addie states it: "My children were of me alone, of the wild blood boiling along the earth, of me and of all that lived; of none and of all" (AILD, 167). That statement is obviously meant to indicate that Addie sees herself as more than an individual woman; she is one participating in a universal cycle. Addie's children become children of all and children of none. She becomes not one human woman, but Mother Earth, anonymous woman and all women. Addie's name also suggests her connection to the earth; Addie might be a feminine derivative of Adam, and Adam means earth.

If one must strain a little to see the connection between Addie's name and nature, the connection is blatant in Addie's daughter, Dewey Dell. In many ways Dewey Dell duplicates her mother's experience. The location of her amorous adventures is also the woods; her illicit child is conceived under circumstances similar to those under which her mother conceived her love child, Jewel. Dewey Dell's emotions are also attuned to natural processes. She says, "I feel like a wet seed wild in the hot blind earth" (AILD, 61). Thus she compares her approaching fruition with the earth's fecundity. She also identifies with other natural gestational creatures. She tells the cow, "You'll have to wait. What you got in you ain't nothing to what I got in me, even if you are a woman too" (AILD, 61). Besides her own perception of her identification with nature, Darl too sees Dewey Dell's female body as interconnected with and superimposed on the landscape: "Squatting, Dewey Dell's wet dress shapes for the dead eyes of three blind men those mammalian ludicrosities which are the horizons and the valleys of the earth" (AILD, 156). As a Mother Earth figure her breasts form the horizons and the valleys of the landscape. Her connection to all women and to woman as fertility and earth goddess is accentuated when Darl describes her leg as "that lever which moves the world; one of that caliper which measures the length and breadth of life" (AILD, 97). Though Dewey Dell is a perverse fertility goddess, one who is trying to abort her seed, she is not successful, and the last image of her in the novel shows her placidly eating a banana, still pregnant. Will she or nil she the continuation of the species is assured.

Faulkner's most florid female characterization is probably Eula Varner. As the incarnation of an earth goddess Eula is probably the most outrageously suprahuman woman in his entire oeuvre. Although she does emerge as almost human in the later books of the Snopes Trilogy, in *The Hamlet* there is little similarity between her and normal human females. She is described as goddess, the female principle, vegetable, and bounteous nature. As a child she is mindless and motionless, carted about and ministered to like a pampered priestess or priceless idol. Like an idol, she seems incapable of responding to her idolization. Her connections to earth are emphasized by her only action, which is the daily consuming of sweet potatoes. In all three books of the Snopes Trilogy, Faulkner lavishes upon her, to the point of absurdity, the imagery of prolific and cataclysmic nature. He does it in his descriptions and his narrators do it in theirs. Ratliff likens her to "a natural phenomenon like a cyclone or a tide-wave . . . " (M, 124). Gavin Stevens describes her as "the sea which in a moment would destroy me, not with any deliberate and calculated sentient wave but simply because I stood there in its way" (T, 93). Her brother, reacting hysterically to the response of the male population to her appearance, screams, "She's just like a dog! Soon as she passes anything in long pants she begins to give off something. You can smell it. You can smell it ten feet away" (H, 112). When the young men in the community approach her at parties they are described as swarming around her like wasps "about the ripe peach which her full damp mouth resembled" (H, 145). The initial description of Eula, when she is not yet 13 years old, dwells on her image as mythic woman, a goddess of fertility incarnate, whose sex organs are the center of her universe:

> On the contrary, her entire appearance suggested some symbology out of the old Dionysic times—honey in sunlight and bursting grapes, the writhen bleeding of the crushed fecundating vine beneath the hard rapacious trampling goathoof. She seemed to be not a living integer of her contemporary scene, but rather to exist in a teeming vacuum in which her days followed one another as though behind sound-proof glass, where she seemed to listen in sullen bemusement, with a weary wisdom heired of all mammalian maturity, to the enlarging of her own organs. (H, 107)

Eula is not only depicted as Mother Earth and Tumultuous Nature, she is also compared at different times in the three books to various other immortals. When she is only 11 years old she is described by Labove, the schoolmaster, as one who "postulated that ungirdled quality of the very goddesses in his Homer and Thucydides: of being at once corrupt and immaculate, at once virgins and the mothers of warriors and of grown men" (H, 128). In *The Town* she is described as "that damned incredible woman that Frenchman's Bend Helen, Semiramis—no: not Helen nor Semiramis: Lilith: the one before Eve herself . . . " (T, 44). Finally in *The Mansion* she is called Venus. Recalling Eula, Charles Mallison says:

> little petty moral conditions like restraint and purity had no more connection with a woman like Mrs. Snopes—or rather a woman like her had no more concern with or even attention for them—mere conventions about what force you use or when or how or where have to do with wars or cyclones. I mean, when a community suddenly discovered that it has the sole ownership of Venus for however long it will last, she cannot, must not be a chaste wife or even faithful mistress whether she is or not or really wants to be or not. (M, 211)

Faulkner himself declared, "She was larger than life, she was too big for this world."[35]

Though the descriptions of her daughter can never quite match those of Eula, for even Gavin Stevens realizes that "very Nature herself would not permit that to occur, permit two of them in a place no larger than Jefferson" (T, 133), Linda Snopes is no ordinary woman. She is, in fact, a combination of three goddesses, the goddesses who tempted Paris: Athena, Aphrodite, and Hera. As a war heroine she takes her place as a modern Athena and she is also Athena-like in her leadership of the forces that finally vanquish Flem Snopes. Her education qualifies her to embody Athena as goddess of wisdom. Whereas Eula spends only five years in school, Linda goes to the university, is continuously fed a reading list by Gavin Stevens, and spends much of her time in Jefferson teaching. Linda as Aphrodite is seen through the sexual fantasies she conjures in the mind of Charles Mallison, who though younger than she, is plagued by carnal thoughts of her before, during, and after his imprisonment in World War II. As goddess of erotic love she loves and is loved by Gavin Stevens as well, but when she decrees a happy marriage to another for him, she assumes a Hera-like role in his life. As Charles sees it, the source of her happiness at the contentment in the Stevens household is the fact that she feels that she invented it. In fact she did.

Besides the suggestion of Linda as modern goddess, there is the ever present nature imagery by which she is described. Like her predecessors she is compared to both plants and animals. Her eyes are described at one point as "kind of the color of wistaria" (T, 189) and at another "as darkest hyacinth, what I have always imagined Homer's hyacinthine sea must have had to look like" (T, 192). Her animallike qualities are projected through her voice and her walk. Once she is deaf, her voice is described as a duck voice. Her walk is compared to a pointer's by both Charles Mallison and Gavin Stevens. Stevens's description is: "She went past us still walking, striding, like the young pointer bitch, the maiden bitch of course, the virgin bitch, immune now in virginity, not scorning the earth, spurning the earth, because she needed it to walk on in that immunity..." (T,132). This collates her description with her mother Eula's. Both are compared to bitch dogs in their younger years. This comparison suggests uncontrollable sexuality and a connection to the Negro woman.

Of course, all of the aforementioned images of woman as an earth or nature goddess, complete with a primitive or pagan sexuality and moral code, are important because it is through this imagery that Faulkner communicated his message about women's indestructibility. For if woman is as the earth, if woman is as matter rather than spirit, then woman, like the earth and matter, is seen as enduring. Civilizations, cities, governments, philosophies, and political maneuvering—all the things that are creations of the male principle—dominate the stage (strut and fret their hour upon the stage) and then are seen no more. The earth, the stage, remains.

The Demeter/Persephone myth is another dominant pattern that Faulkner used to transmit his sense of woman's indestructibility. Carvell Collins, Richard P. Adams, and Walter Brylowski have all written about Faulkner's use of this myth. Collins concludes that whereas Joyce and Freud were strong influences in the writing of *The Sound and the Fury*, James Frazer's *The Golden Bough* is a primary source for *As I Lay Dying*. Collins's thesis is that Faulkner presents "Addie, Dewey Dell, and Cora in a detailed and significant parallel with the Greeks' three-in-one goddess Demeter-Persephone-Kore."[36] Collins makes many ingenious comparisons between characters and events in the myth and in the novel, concluding that Addie is an inverted Demeter and Dewey Dell an inverse comparison to Persephone. He never does explain how Cora fits into the pattern. The only connection I can see is a linguistic one;

Cora sounds like Kore. However, in Greek Kore means maiden and the term is used to refer to Persephone. Cora can hardly be seen as maiden in *As I Lay Dying*. She is more like a witness, such as Hecate was, but a witness who misinterprets the meaning of everything, a nice comic inversion consistent with the way Faulkner played with mythic patterns.

According to Richard P. Adams, Faulkner used the Persephone paradigm in a number of novels with "*Sanctuary* as the strongest example of its use."[37] Adams's witty explication of Faulkner's appropriation of the myth is limited to showing its use as organizing structure or form. Adams points out that the Persephone myth is but one of many myths at work in Faulknerian characterizations, symbolism, and plot patterns. Adams's discussion of the Persephone myth as one, and he is careful to underline that it is but one, of many mythic patterns that Faulkner used is important for a fuller perception of Faulkner's works, but he, like Collins, stops short of analyzing the thematic significance of Faulkner's use of the myth.

Brylowski, distinguishing among the various levels of myth apparent in Faulkner's works, calls the comparison of Caddy Compson and Eula Varner to Persephone the "simple" level of myth, that level which is allusion and analogy.[38] He sees, for example, the rape of Temple Drake as analogous to the rape of Persephone. In Brylowski's interpretation of *Sanctuary*, Horace Benbow becomes Demeter, the grieving mother, searching for her daughter, a curious interpretation even at a "simple" level.

Brylowski, Adams, and Collins are instructive, but their explications do not explore the full implications of Faulkner's use of the Demeter/Persephone myth as not only a pattern for plot structure, but as a paradigm for an essential truth of existence, the significance of female endurance and continuity. In the stories of Caddy Compson and her daughter Quentin, Addie and Dewey Dell Bundren, and Eula Varner Snopes and Linda Snopes, Faulkner presents varying rhapsodies on the theme from the Eleusinian mysteries, all of which sing of the perpetuation of life through the reunion of mother and daughter.

Frazer, whom Faulkner most certainly read, saw Demeter and Persephone as personifications of corn, who in the course of religious evolution also became symbols for rebirth: "Above all, the thought of the seed buried in the earth in order to spring up to new and higher life readily suggested a comparison with human destiny, and strengthened the hope that for man too the grave may be the beginning of a better and happier existence in some brighter world unknown."[39]

More recent scholars have interpreted the myth in similar ways. C. Kerenyi's book *Eleusis: Archetypal Image of Mother and Daughter* is a study of the implications of the Demeter/Persephone myth. Kerenyi explains that divinities are best understood as eternal forms, the great world-realities; the reason for their mightiness is their truth. That truth, however, is a relative one, one that exists delicately balanced in "a border-line situation," analogous to the paradoxical character of reality. An example of this is the figures of the gods. "In Apollo sublimest clarity and the darkness of death face one another, perfectly poised and equal on a borderline; in Dionysus, life and death."[40] The idea of Artemis is found in the untamedness of young animals and equally in the terror of birth. She is at once chaste goddess of the hunt and protector of women in childbirth. Though this seems a paradox, Kerenyi suggests that such paradoxes are the very essence of the "bud-like" quality of myth in that they transmit the sense of something unopened like a bud, something that will unfold and enlarge. The myth of Persephone embodies just such a borderline situation or budlike form of two extremes balanced against each other. "One of the forms (daughter with mother) appears as life; the other (young girl with husband) as death."[41]

Another of the "bud" possibilities of the myth is in the triune form of the Kore, the maiden. Athena and Artemis are with Persephone when she is carried away by Hades. In this combination they can be seen as alter egos or other aspects of the Kore. Athena is the intellectual and spiritual Kore and Artemis is the huntress, at home in the natural world, whereas Persephone is completely passive. She is picking flowers when she is raped. The flowers were of the heavily scented and stupefying variety, and Faulkner often uses the pervasive scent of honeysuckle and other strongly scented flowers as sensory metaphors for female sexuality.

The paradoxical position of Persephone is also seen in the fact that though she is worshipped as Kore and corn maiden, she is also worshipped as Queen of the Dead. The rape of the bride can also be an allegory for death; lost maidenhood and the crossing of the borders of Hades are allegorically analogous.[42] Loss of maidenhood is often the crossing into the land of the underworld for Faulkner's Persephones. Psychological critics make much of the fact that Faulkner's fictional "heart's darling" is a young girl seen at the time of her developing sexuality, a sexuality which dooms her to exile from her family. Faulkner's own feelings of ambiguity about the maturation of female sexuality were communicated in a number of ways. Meta Carpenter writes of his need to transform her into a young girl, ignoring her previous marriage and adult experiences. As he grew older he became involved with younger and younger women.[43]

Still another of the "bud-like" situations contained in the myth is the presence of Hecate in most versions of the story. According to the Homeric myth, Hecate is in her cave and hears the cries of Persephone as she is being ravished. Hecate thus becomes a double for Demeter who also hears the cries. In some versions of the story, Hecate performs some of the actions that are attributed to Demeter in others. Thus the three goddesses are joined: "A compact group, a triad of unmistakable individuals, this is how the hymn shows the three goddesses: Mother, Daughter, and the moon-goddess, Hecate."[44] And those three, representing the tripartite woman, are another basic paradigm for Faulkner's indestructible women.

For the purpose of exploring how Faulkner used the Demeter/ Persephone myth as a pattern for female continuity, I will first concentrate on only two of the triad, the mother and the daughter. Later I will discuss Faulkner's use of the indomitable crone figure or witness. The unity of Demeter and her daughter was the central content of the Eleusinian mysteries. In order for life on earth to flourish, they must be reunited. The pictorial representations of the time show them as a double figure, sometimes indistinguishable from each other. "Persephone is, above all, her mother's Kore; without her, Demeter would not be *Meter*."[45] Demeter and Kore, mother and daughter, are symbolic extensions of the feminine consciousness, extending it both backwards and forwards. As they merge into one, the myth suggests "that every mother contains her daughter in herself and every daughter her mother, and that every woman extends backwards into her mother and forwards into her daughter."[46] In this way the myth has strong implications of continuity and immortality.

Erich Neumann sees the myth as the mystery of the endless renewal of the Eternal Woman, for as Kore is restored to Demeter, she becomes identical with her, and so as each daughter ceases to be Maiden, she then becomes Mother, and "the mystery of the Feminine is susceptible to endless renewal."[47]

Faulkner's works demonstrate his sensitivity to the "bud-like" qualities of myth, the borderline, the balance of extremities at the heart of the paradox of the mythological idea. He continuously plays on these paradoxes, developing ambiguities, inverting patterns to demonstrate the flexibility of the paradigm. Such is his use of the Demeter/Persephone myth. In his inversion, when both the mother and daughter are present in the story, it is the mother, not the daughter, who must undergo the trip to the underworld or "death" to insure the endurance of the daughter. Faulkner acknowledged this kind of literary tampering openly: "The writer, as I say, never forgets that [what he has read], he stores it away—he has no morals—and when he needs it, he reaches around and drags it out, and if it doesn't quite fit what he wants to say he'll probably change it just a little."[48] And change it he does. However, since mother and daughter are as one in the myth, Faulkner's inversion is not so much a serious violation of the integrity of the myth as an inventive use of its budlike possibilities.

Faulkner's earliest use of this inverted myth is in *The Sound and the Fury*. Caddy must exile herself to insure Quentin II's future. In effect she, like Persephone, becomes the bride of the lord of the underworld, a Nazi officer's mistress. The oneness of Caddy and Quentin II is underscored in many ways.

Jason calls them both "bitches," stating emphatically on another occasion that Quentin II is "just like her mother." Caddy and Quentin II both escape the Compson domain of sickness and sterility in similar ways, by climbing out of the window to assert their sexuality. Quentin II, though she does not know her mother, identifies with her and against Jason. Rather than wear a dress bought with Jason's money, she is ready to tear it off. This is not a pose, though Jason thinks it might be initially. "Then I saw that she really was trying to tear it, to tear it right off her" (SF, 233). Both women are treated similarly by Jason; he controls them through blackmail. The merger of the two is also accomplished in the mind of their creator. In a 1956 interview with Jean Stein, Faulkner assesses *The Sound and the Fury* as the story of two lost women. Explaining the meaning of the muddy drawers, he said, "And then I realized the symbolism of the soiled pants, and that image was replaced by one of a fatherless and motherless girl climbing down the rainpipe to escape the only home she had, where she had never been offered love or affection or understanding." Quentin II's image replaces or is superimposed on Caddy's in Faulkner's mind, and the soiled pants are replaced by the soiled girl.

Though Quentin II repeats the tragic circumstances of her mother's life, as in the myth spring and summer give way to fall and winter, there is a strong implication that though she runs away, she is not defeated or destroyed. After a period in the underworld each year, Persephone is returned. In one interview, Faulkner even suggested the rejuvenation of Quentin II in a future book.[49] He did revive Temple Drake, another of his Persephones who undergoes a time in the underworld only to be resurrected to motherhood and redemption. Even without this external evidence, the pattern of rejuvenation is implicit in the novel itself. Quentin II triumphs by her defeat of Jason; and she does this in the only way he understands, by taking "his" money. Her route of escape is suggestive symbolically of life and fruition; she climbs down a blossoming pear tree. In the Demeter/Persephone myth the image of the flower and fruit combine as they do in the image of the blossoming pear tree. Quentin II escapes the sterile and love-destroying atmosphere of the decaying Compson household as Persephone escapes from the underworld.

The perpetuation of female generations can also be deduced from another mother/daughter pair in *The Sound and the Fury*. Dilsey's daughter Frony seems destined to continue in her mother's caretaking role. The men in the Gibson family may be troublesome, but not Frony. She cares about her mother, hoping that the Easter sermon will "give her the comfort en de unburdenin." Dilsey is Demeter-like in her ability to love all living creatures, making no distinctions among her children, even when she is told that some people are talking about her bringing Benjy to church. Dilsey is also, in deed if not in fact, more of a mother to the Compson family than Caroline Compson. Another way of reading the novel posits Dilsey in the Demeter role and Caddy in the role of her Kore. Dilsey, like Demeter, is a provider of sustenance. She is the one who "feeds" both the Compson and Gibson families. Her image as the provider of nourishment is emphasized when she is described as standing like a cow in the rain. Like Demeter, Dilsey grieves for her "lost" daughter. Symbolically, that daughter is returned to her in the person of Caddy's daughter Quentin II. She has her for a season, and then loses her again, just as in the myth Persephone must return to the underworld after a period with her mother.

Caddy's ability to return from the underworld, her ability to endure, is signaled a number of ways. Although she has been deprived of her daughter, she has not been destroyed. She continues to provide for that daughter, sending money for Quentin II's maintenance. And Quentin II "rescues" that money when she escapes, symbolically returning to her mother in the person of herself what is rightfully theirs. The last image of Caddy in the novel suggests luxury, money, and sunlight, in a background of mountains, palms, cypresses, and the sea, all symbols of nature and beauty. Though she is in the paradoxical situation of being with a lord of the underworld, she is also seen as a survivor. She has endured family deaths, cruelty, and lost dreams, and stands in the sunshine. Her hell has provided her daughter's sustenance.

Addie and Dewey Dell Bundren also fit into the Demeter/Persephone archetypal pattern. Numerous critics have explored the Earth Mother imagery that is used to characterize both of these women.[50] In one of the images of the novel that most specifically suggests Dewey Dell as an incarnation of Persephone, she describes herself as a "wet seed wild in the hot-blind earth." As in the case of Caddy and Quentin, there is a fusion of mother and daughter. Both engender illicit children in the woods; both are nurturers, serving their family of men. In Dewey Dell's perception, Addie must die, in this case be literally consigned to the underworld, so that she can have her chance. Ironically, Dewey Dell wants not to sustain life, but to abort it. In keeping with the ironic sense of humor that is the dominant tone of *As I Lay Dying*, Dewey Dell's trip through hell will sustain life. In the myth, Persephone is raped by Hades, Lord of the Underworld. In *As I Lay Dying,* Dewey Dell is taken advantage of by both her father Anse when he takes the money Lafe gave her and by the druggist's assistant who literally and figuratively takes her to the underworld, a cellar.

Throughout the nightmarish occurrences of Dewey Dell's trip through and to Hell, she acts in many nurturing and life-sustaining ways. She is first seen fanning Addie on her deathbed. She is next seen preparing food for the family. She cares for Cash when he is hurt. She takes over the care of Vardaman, who even accompanies her to her rendezvous with the druggist's assistant.

Just as the Persephone of the myth is not as active a character as her mother Demeter, so none of Faulkner's Persephones quite measure up to their mothers. Linda Snopes may be the exception, but then there is no other woman in all of Faulkner who measures up to Linda Snopes. Like the Persephone of the myth, Dewey Dell is mostly passive. Demeter searches all over heaven and earth for her daughter; her grief lays waste the land; she effects the rites and ceremonies to commemorate the reunion. Persephone is merely victim, the acted upon. Yet it is she who is the embodiment of spring, she who is the renewal; it is her return which is celebrated. Thus Addie, in the active role, "takes" Anse, sets up elaborate codes of word and deed, aloneness and unaloneness, sets into motion the revenge of the journey to Jefferson. But it is through Dewey Dell that the "duty to the alive," the preservation of the species, is effected.

Howe dismisses Dewey Dell as "vegetable," "concerned only with her ease," a depiction which is hardly borne out by her actions.[51] Perhaps "vegetative" would be a better description since it would convey a sense of her fertility. Fiedler sees her as malevolently destructive; "Faulkner's dewiest dells turn out to be destroyers rather than redeemers, quicksands disguised as sacred groves."[52] One despises her for her inertness, one for her aggression. Stonesifer has come to her defense as the guardian of her mother's decree.[53] What none of these gentlemen have noted is that, at the end of the book, Dewey Dell is the only Bundren who represents possibilities for the renewal of life. Cash is crippled, and if he hasn't shown much interest in women prior to the funeral trip, he is not likely to begin at that point. Jewel's sexual interest has been his horse, which he has now lost. Darl is in an insane asylum, hardly a fruitful possibility. Vardaman is still a child. Yet, one of the final images in the novel is of Dewey Dell, still pregnant, munching on a banana, an image rich with implications of continuity and renewal.

Faulkner's use of the Demeter/Persephone pattern in the Snopes trilogy develops not only the thematic implications but also clearly explores the moral dimensions of the myth. The forces of evil, death, impotence, and destruction are personified in Snopesism, against which Gavin Stevens, V.K. Ratliff, and Charles Mallison have joined forces. Like Popeye, Faulkner's earlier incarnation of Pluto/Hades, Flem Snopes is an impotent bridegroom from the underworld. Popeye's Persephone, Temple Drake, is not fertile while in his care. Her fecundity is not realized until her rehabilitation in *Requiem for a Nun*. In *The Hamlet*, Eula Varner is already pregnant when Flem Snopes marries her. Because of Flem's impotence and the lovelessness of their relationship, their marriage is sterile, a symbolic Land of the Dead.

In Eula, Demeter and Persephone are one. She is Persephone who is carried away by the Lord of the Underworld, but she is also the great Earth Goddess who is worshipped wherever she is known. Ratliff calls his room the Eula Varner room, but Charles Mallison says it is more like a "Shrine," and Ratliff concedes that it is indeed (M, 232). Labove takes on the qualities of a priest as he is engulfed in his worship of Eula. The narrator characterizes

Labove's designation as "professor" by the other characters in the novel as a distinction like the title of "reverend." He is expected not to drink or curse (H, 126). He becomes monklike in his devotion: "He was the virile anchorite of old time" (H, 134).

As the pattern of Persephone's removal from her mother is repeated every year, and Demeter, after the blossoming of spring and summer, sorrows through the coldness of winter, so Eula becomes the sorrowing goddess because of the loss of her daughter. Just as Persephone is bound to Pluto because of the pomegranate seed she ate while in the underworld, so Linda is bound to Flem because of the lie of her parentage. In order for Linda to have her chance for happiness, to escape Flem, Eula thinks that she must die. In terms of the mythic pattern, the Earth (in this case the Earth Mother) must die so that spring can return. This and other death/rebirth imagery abounds in the Snopes Trilogy.

The oneness of Eula and Linda, mother and daughter, is underscored in various manners. Linda is repeatedly seen as Eula reborn. The three point-of-view characters, through whose perception the story is told, V.K. Ratliff, Gavin Stevens, and Charles Mallison, all switch their adoration from mother to daughter. At the end of the final book, when Linda leaves Jefferson, the theme of continuity is articulated by Ratliff. He says, "I don't know if she's already got a daughter stashed out somewhere, or if she jest aint got around to one yet. But when she does I jest hope for Old Lang Zyne's sake she dont never bring it back to Jefferson. You done already been through two Eula Varners and I dont think you can stand another one" (M, 434).

The implications of this statement are in keeping with the message of the myth. The image is one of a continuously renewable line of mothers and daughters: Demeter and Persephone reunited anew for each year and each generation. Ratliff does not suggest a male child and in terms of both Faulkner's use of the myth and his other symbolism in the trilogy, this is significant. Sally Page's study of Faulkner's women argues for a pattern of life-nourishing representatives of the female principle, particularly in the maternal role, in opposition to life-destroying representatives of the male principle. David Williams, though his reading of the significance of Linda's character is less positive, agrees that "Linda suggests the archetypal feminine's potential for re-emergence."[54] The Snopes domain—the land of death and destruction, the land of the Lord of the Underworld—is male; the earth—the land of fecundity and motion—is female and it is the return of the daughter which renews it. As Gavin Stevens explains: "So that was not the first time I ever thought how apparently all Snopeses are male, as if the mere and simple incident of woman's divinity precluded Snopesishness and made it paradox" (T,136).

Besides the indestructible females who because of their earthlike qualities endure and besides the indestructible mother-daughter combinations who provide hope through renewal, there is still another indestructible type in Faulkner's works. Perhaps indomitable would be a better word to describe this type, which completes the female cycle, the tripartite woman who is maiden, mother, and crone. In describing one of his indestructible crones, Faulkner speaks of her "actual stardom in the role of the matriarch, arbitrating from the fireside corner of the crone the pride and destiny of her family" (A,A!, 69). The woman as crone appears regularly in Faulkner's fiction and more often than not she functions as an aspect of his primitivism. The connection of woman and Negro both as more primitive and therefore more sexual beings has already been established. In Faulkner's credo of female endurance, fecundity is an important factor, but when he deals with women past the age of reproduction, the credo is enlarged to include them also. Whereas fertile women can insure the survival of the species through their fecundity, the crones play an important role in nurturing those who survive and in many instances providing sustenance. Like Hecate, they also serve as witnesses, communicating the values. Thus these indomitable crones are mothers in deed if not in blood. However, they do not accomplish this alone. Generally, they band with blacks and children, other "primitives," to not only survive, but to prevail.

Intruder in the Dust and *The Unvanquished* are two novels that embody this brand of Faulknerian primitivism. Miss Habersham, Granny Rosa Millard, and Miss Jenny DuPre are composites of Faulkner's "old undefeated spinster aunts" and the seemingly fragile but steel-spined southern woman. Small but indomitable women were significant in Faulkner's personal life. He once remarked that his mother and his mammy didn't weigh 200 pounds between them, but that they easily handled a house roaring with five men.[55] Of the three fictional characters, neither Miss Habersham nor Miss Jenny DuPre are biological mothers, but they are matriarchal figures. Miss Habersham is a 70-year-old spinster. However, though she may not have been a mother literally, she does function as a provider; she raises chickens and vegetables and peddles them around the town. Margaret Mallison, Chick's mother, amplifies the image of woman as the one who provides and sustains. She and Paralee (Alek's mother) feed and care for the justice seekers, the two boys Chick and Alek, and then Maggie goes to the jail to sit in the jailhouse door with Miss Habersham because the white male supremacy code would prevent even a lynch mob from running over two white ladies to get at Lucas Beauchamp.

In this novel, preventing a miscarriage of justice is left to the women and the children, Miss Habersham and Margaret Mallison, Alek Sanders and

Chick Mallison. One is reminded of Giradoux's madwoman of Chaillot who proclaims that there is nothing so wrong with the world that it can't be set straight by a good woman in the course of an afternoon, a vision acceptable in fantasy but questionable in the turbulent, blood-soaked land that was the prototype for Yoknapatawpha. What transforms this fantasy into reality for Faulkner is his special combination of sexism, racism, and primitivism. In his characterization woman as more childlike and more intuitive than man is a natural ally for others of her kind. Miss Habersham articulates the idea when she explains, "Lucas knew it would take a child—or an old woman like me: someone not concerned with probability, with evidence" (IITD, 89). Lucas, the primitive Negro, chooses not his lawyer, but his fellow primitives to help him. Whereas the black man and the white man are not of the same species, the black man, the black woman and the white woman and children are. "Of course. Naturally he wouldn't tell your uncle. He's a Negro and your uncle's a man," Miss Habersham explains, and for Chick, "what Miss Habersham was paraphrasing was simple truth" (IITD, 89).

Femaleness does not have the same color distinctions as maleness. This is especially true when it comes to the reproductive role. Black or white, once a woman is a mother, she cannot be overcome. When Gavin Stevens offers to try to convince Margaret and Paralee to let the boys stay out of school, Chick's response is "You're just my uncle" (IITD, 122). Gavin counters, "I'm worse than that. I'm just a man." He has little hope for success because it does not matter if a mother is black or white; women operate by their own criteria. "The same condition obtains there; motherhood doesn't seem to have any pigment in its skin" (IITD, 123). While fatherhood does not create any kind of bond between black men and white men, motherhood is a universal that transcends the temporal considerations of race and geography.

The women in *Intruder in the Dust* are not only allies, they are also invincible. Gavin Stevens explains to Chick about his mother and all women, "Dont you know she's tougher than you and me both just as old Habersham was tougher than you and Alek Sanders put together" (IITD, 106). This attitude is repeated by Gavin throughout the novel and since his ideas are not contradicted by the actions in the story, one assumes that Faulkner shared this attitude. Gavin explains women's ability to endure saying, "Just remember that they can stand anything, accept any fact (its only men who burk at facts)... " (IITD, 107). Chick and his uncle both come to the conclusion that "you not only couldn't beat them, but you couldn't even find the battlefield in time to admit defeat before they moved it again" (IITD, 123). By the end of the novel, Chick, who is making the transition from child to man, concludes that women "couldn't really stand anything except tragedy and poverty and physical pain" (IITD, 208).

A number of cultural and regional stereotypes as well as forthright primitivism are at work in this novel's naive and optimistic message. Women,

Negroes, and children are depicted as intuitive, natural, and elemental peers who will save the world when man's creations, such as the judicial system, go askew. Women and Negroes are the hope for the future because of "that capacity to survive and absorb and endure and still be steadfast" (IITD, 204). And Miss Habersham, indestructible, indomitable, undefeated spinster, like Hecate, is there both as an actor and as a witness to restore justice.

Granny Rosa Millard personifies "the unvanquished" in the book of the same name. Granny is the reigning matriarch of the Sartoris clan and while the men are off playing at another of man's foolish games, war, Granny sees to the more important business of human survival. True to her image as the great Mother Goddess, Granny provides for the whole territory. In order to provide for her "children" she must lie and she explains the necessity for this sin in her prayer, "I sinned for the sake of food and clothes for Your own creatures who would not help themselves—for children who had given their fathers, for wives who had given their husbands, for old people who had given their sons..." (U, 167). She even takes the patriarchal god to task for not taking care of these items himself, thereby creating the necessity for her doing it. While the men are off "strutting and swaggering" and "swashbuckling," as Miss Jenny DuPre later calls it, Rosa Millard, small, fragile, female, and aged, protects the home and the hearth and the children, sustaining those things that will be necessary for future survival. Through all her hardship and suffering, she endures. As her grandson Bayard sees her, "during those four years she hadn't got any older or weaker, but just littler and littler and straighter and straighter and more and more indomitable..." (U, 163).

The myth of the fragile southern belle with the spine of steel is the underlying image here. It is expressed by such a variety of characters that it becomes inextricable from Faulkner's own voice, especially since he often made similar pronouncements. The Yankee lieutenant who has to deal with Miss Rosa is well aware of the myth:

> I'd rather engage Forrest's whole brigade every morning for six months than spend the same length of time trying to protect the United State property from defenseless Southern women and niggers and children. Defenseless! Defenseless! God help the North if Davis and Lee had ever thought of the idea of forming a brigade of grandmothers and nigger orphans and invading us with it. (U, 163)

Ab Snopes, too, pays tribute to Miz Rosa's indomitable qualities: "What I wonder is, if somebody hadn't better tell Abe Lincoln to look out for General Grant against Miz Rosa Millard" (U, 140). But perhaps the best summary of Faulkner's attitude toward the indestructibility of women is in Aunt Louisa's letter. "But it is not myself that I am thinking of since I am a woman, a mother, a Southern woman, and it has been our lot during the last four years to learn to bear anything" (U, 218-19).

The combination of children, blacks, and women as primitive saviors operates in *The Unvanquished* as it did in *Intruder in the Dust*. As in *Intruder in the Dust*, a white child, Bayard, and a black child, Ringo, band with an indomitable crone, in this case to outwit the Yankees and provide for their people. As a team they are unbelievably successful. It is only when a white man is added to the formula that the whole scheme collapses and disaster strikes. The death of Granny is caused by their association with Ab Snopes, Snopesism being the metaphor for the destructive male principle.[56] Granny's indestructibility is evidenced even in death, for her work is not destroyed. Her funeral is attended by all those she has provided for, "the old men and the women and the children, and the niggers." And the preacher testifies to her indomitable spirit in a eulogy which, like Miz Rosa, is short and practical. Even in death her spirit is seen as nurturing: "And I reckon that God has already seen to it that there are men, women, and children, black, white, yellow, and red, waiting for her to tend and worry over" (U, 180). The great Mother Goddess does not differentiate by sex or race. Just as she cared for her children in life, so in death, the preacher, speaking for her practical sense, tells all those attending the funeral:

> And so you folks go home. Some of you ain't come far, and you came that distance in carriages with tops. But most of you didn't and it's by the grace of Rosa Millard that you didn't come on foot. I'm talking to you. You have wood to cut and split, at least. And what do you reckon Rosa Millard would say about you standing around here, keeping old folks and children out here in the rain? (U, 180)

The people have the mules Granny has provided; thus her caring for them continues. All of her children have been sustained in various ways and when John Sartoris returns from war, he also finds his plantation intact. Granny's work endures for she has preserved the Sartoris legacy for future generations.

As in *Intruder in the Dust*, there are two main indestructible women in *Sartoris*. Between them, they manage to play all three roles of the tripartite woman: maiden, mother, and crone. At the beginning of the novel Narcissa is a maiden; at the end she is a mother. Miss Jenny DuPre is the unvanquishable old lady.

The flower imagery that is used to portray Narcissa is reminiscent of the flowers that are connected with Persephone. "Narcissa wore gray and her eyes were violet, and in her face was the tranquil repose of lilies" (Sar, 31). Not only is she presented in floral visual images, but her very being permeates the air with a strong floral scent: "Her constant presence fills the room like the odor of jasmine" (Sar, 176). Her name, of course, is another instance of Faulkner's use of names to suggest the character of their bearer.

As a maiden, Narcissa shrinks from the blatant sexuality of women such as Belle Mitchell. Like so many characters in Faulkner, Narcissa makes the connection of female sexuality with the soil, saying that she somehow feels that Belle is dirty. Miss Jenny, who has been a wife, counters, "All women are, if that's what you mean."

The positive powers of the female earth principle are indicated by the one peaceful period in Bayard Sartoris's chaotic search for his doom. His one moment of contentment comes when he works the land. While he does the nurturant things—planting, tending, and caring for the plants—he is held in a hiatus from his destruction-seeking path. As he falls into the rhythm of the earth's processes, he is, for the moment, saved. "He had been so neatly tricked by the earth, that ancient Delilah ... " (Sar, 204). The metaphor here is of the earth as woman, that woman a temptress. This temptress, however, leads man into a positive, healthy life. When Bayard turns from the earth and nurturant activities, he goes back to his death-seeking ways. The curative powers of Mother Earth are another illustration of Faulkner's primitivism.

The indestructible crone in this novel is Miss Jenny DuPre, who has been married to another of the Sartoris family's death-seeking males. Miss Jenny, indomitable old fire-eater that she is, is fed up with man's ridiculous posturing and infirmities. She especially has little patience with man's reaction to war, which she considers the epitome of the male animal's absurd inventions. Viewing all the psychological trauma men suffer as a result of war, Miss Jenny says, "I'll declare men can't seem to stand anything" (Sar, 53). In her opinion, it is men who devise the wars for no good reason, and therefore she feels they should have the good grace not to make nuisances of themselves when they return from their foolishness. In Miss Jenny's opinion it is the women who really suffer:

> Do you think a man could sit day after day and month after month in a house miles from nowhere and spend the time between casualty lists tearing up bedclothes and window curtains and table linen to make lint, and watching sugar and flour and meat dwindling away, and using pine knots for light because there aren't any candles and no candlesticks to put 'em in if there were, and hiding in nigger cabins while drunken Yankee generals set fire to the house your great-great-grandfather built and you and all your folks were born in? Don't talk to me about men suffering in war. (Sar, 53)

Her attitude is not unlike the one expressed by Euripides's indomitable women in *Lysistrata*. The men go off to war, swaggering, strutting, and frightening old women in the marketplace; the women stay home and suffer, their lives dribbling away in the manless state of maiden or widow.

Narcissa wonders at Miss Jenny's enduring qualities. Thinking of her she sits, "admiring more than ever that indomitable spirit that born with a woman's body ... had seen, as in a nightmare ... the foundations of her life swept away and had her roots torn bodily from the soil where her forefathers sleep ... " (Sar, 357). Narcissa realizes the hardships and horrors Miss Jenny has lived through and endured. She contrasts that with male courage and concludes, "how much finer that gallantry . . . that uncomplaining steadfastness of those . . . women than the fustian and useless glamour of the men . . ." (Sar, 358).

Miss Jenny is indeed a remarkable woman. She goes careening around with Bayard in his new automobile at breakneck speeds. Men's gadgets do not frighten her. She vanquishes the officious nurse who would detain her because she has no appointment with the doctor. Miss Jenny cannot be bothered with useless formalities. She is held in awe by the people of the town. The sheriff says, when he jails Bayard on Miss Jenny's instructions, "I ruther make Bayard mad than Miss Jenny" (Sar, 159).

At the end of the novel, all the men have managed to be destroyed in one manner or another. Bayard has found his long-sought-for death in an airplane. Old Bayard has died of a heart attack during one of his grandson's hair-raising automobile exploits. Old Simon, the faithful black retainer, is found with his head smashed in. Even Horace has found a metaphorical destruction: he married Belle. This would not seem such a horrible fate except that Horace feels as though Belle were enveloping him, "like a motionless and cloying sea in which he watched himself drown" (Sar, 257). All that are left are the two indestructible women and the baby to signal hope for a new generation.

Marriage to the male is allegorically the descent into Hell in the myth. In what is suggestive of a scene that might have followed Persephone's return from Hades's domain, Miss Jenny asks Narcissa if she would marry Bayard all over again. Narcissa's answer is, "Don't you know I would?" To preserve the race Narcissa must go through a hellish marriage, and then be left alone with only Miss Jenny to sustain her. Both women understand this positive function of woman. "Again there was silence between them, in which without words they sealed their hopeless pact with that fine and passive courage of woman." In this passage Faulkner as narrator reinforces the theme, articulated by various characters in the novel, of woman's courage and endurance.

The problem of Faulkner's attitude toward women is one that has continually perplexed his readers and provoked an abundance of critical reaction. The call for papers at the twelfth annual "Faulkner and Yoknapatawpha" conference on the subject of Faulkner and women inspired 84 submissions. There has even been a dissertation devoted to *An Annotated Bibliography of Criticism of Women Characters in William Faulkner's Criticism.*[57] Cleanth Brooks calls it "the most difficult of all questions in Faulkner, Faulkner's attitude toward women."[58]

The problem of trying to come to terms with Faulkner's female characters has caused a number of critics to seek categories by which to analyze them. Miller finds two categories: earth mothers and ghosts.[59] Kerr concludes that Faulkner's rejection of the southern ideal or what she calls southern gyneolatry accounts for his two attitudes toward women: rejection of those who personify it and sympathy for those who rebel against it or live naturally outside it.[60] Jackson's categories are "demon-nun and angel-witch."[61]

Obviously, the question of how Faulkner viewed women will not be answered by arriving at any number of categories, no matter how useful and interesting those approaches might be. Nor is the type of the indestructible woman meant to be used as a touchstone by which to judge Faulkner's attitude toward all women. The women in his works are diverse and his attitudes toward them are by no means monotypic. The delineation of such a type in his works is meant, among other things, to suggest one way in which the articulated optimism of Faulkner's Nobel Prize speech is communicated in his fiction, to identify a type which personifies one of Faulkner's dominant attitudes toward women and to suggest the similarities between his attitudes and those of two of his distinguished peers.

The character type of an indestructible woman transcends most categories based on antipathies because of the mythic paradigm that underlies her development. It is also derived from the combination of Faulkner's philosophical primitivism and subjective masculinism, an inability to see woman as anything but a different species. The primitivism in Faulkner concludes that that which is simple and natural will survive; those who are more attuned to life's processes will endure. Woman as *other,* as matter instead of mind, as manifestation of the Earth Goddess instead of the individual being, is organically attuned with the motion of life and thereby more enduring. But this primitive being is also of an earthiness and physicality which may offend the fastidiousnous of the more spiritually inclined male. The way Faulkner's indestructible females are often characterized reflects an awe that is born of reaction to their awfulness, in both senses of the word. Traditional morality has nothing to do with it, nor has a sense of what is customarily regarded as normal or abnormal. The characterizations are born of the same kind of fascination and repugnance that one experiences in the presence of many examples of the way that nature insures survival, such as the black widow devouring her mate or larvae feeding off of the bodies of their parents.

As for the pathology of the Faulknerian world, many critics have commented upon the profusion of horrors that inundate Faulkner's novels and short stories. Edith Hamilton, best known for her work in classical mythology, articulates the connections between the myth of Yoknapatawpha and traditional mythology. Her evaluation is not a pretty one. According to Hamilton, "Mr. Faulkner's novels are about ugly people in an ugly land."[62]

The land is cursed; the people are doomed. It is not unlike the plains of Troy and the halls of Mycenae. On the subject of Faulkner's women, Hamilton has some trenchant observations:

> And his women? No one adjective or two can describe them. I confess that his attitude to them puzzles me. I know nothing like it in literature outside of "The Golden Bough." Frazer's account of the way some primitive tribes feel toward young women, the mixture of violent attraction and equally violent repulsion, is just what Mr. Faulkner feels. Young women are not really human to him.[63]

Hamilton underscores the lack of humanity in many of Faulkner's characters, especially the women. This results, she says, from the fact that he uses his characters as "volitionless servants of fatality." Hamilton expresses what this reader has often felt but been hard put to explain: the special gift that Faulkner has for making an experience come alive brilliantly without creating a feeling of either empathy or sympathy for the character involved, so that it is easy to detach the emotion from the embodiment of it.[64] This also contributes to the mythic quality of the works.

Hamilton's article expresses consternation at Faulkner's Nobel Prize acceptance speech, which she sees as a condemnation of the work which won him the prize. She says, "In his books he reminds us only of the futility of all things human and the certain defeat of all men's struggles."[65] Indeed, though Faulkner does present the struggles of individuals working in a temporal context as often futile, he is also consistently conscious of the "immemorial earth" which is the backdrop against which all the individual agonies are exercised. The earth, and those characters who do not seek to control or ravish it, those who are attuned to its cycles, do prevail. It is only the actions of those individuals who struggle against "motion" which are futile.

Those individuals who live in tune with nature, "the primitives," are the subject of considerable critical interpretation. Sometimes women are included in this class, sometimes they are not. Geismar, in a work subsequent to his previously quoted *Writers in Crisis*, points out Faulkner's shortcomings as a writer while still expressing admiration for his treatment of "the typical phobias and deep haunting fears and obsessions of the cultural background whose supreme literary voice he really is."[66] Among these phobias and obsessions, according to Geismar, is a fear and hatred of the woman and an analogous fear and hatred of the Negro. Geismar explains that Faulkner is only comfortable with Negroes who are the stereotype of the faithful retainer. He does not make the corollary observation that Faulkner was only comfortable with women who played their traditional roles as grandmothers, mothers, wives, and daughters. He posits the idea that Faulkner denies this hatred and fear by projecting onto women and Negroes an image of "endurance," of being "better than we are" which is actually a response to the guilt Faulkner feels about his old prejudices and superstitions.[67] Geismar says he is not fooled at all by what he calls the "lofty new morality" of the Nobel Prize speech.

Melvin Backman's "Sickness and Primitivism: A Dominant Pattern in William Faulkner's Work" delineates the overwhelming number of sick, self-tormented, and death-seeking figures in Faulkner's works. Backman sees that, "Set against these figures of sickness are the primitives, who are free from enervating inner conflicts and who pursue simple direct lives.... They are unthinkingly in accord with the scheme of the universe."[68] This statement conjures up visions of Eula Varner, unaware of the turmoil around her, placidly responding to the enlarging of her organs or Addie Bundren who responds to the voice of the land. Backman marks the Negroes "who qualify by their capacity to endure stoically, and the idiots and morons who qualify by their very insulation from the lusts and cruelty and shattered idealism of modern man" as members of Faulkner's redemptive primitive class.[69] However, he fails to classify women as part of the primitive group. He sees Dilsey and Benjy as balances to the sickness of Quentin's world and the ugliness of Jason's, but fails to mention Caddy, who is a main source of love for Benjy. Caddy is also loving toward Dilsey, Quentin, Mr. Compson, and her daughter. Nor does Backman note that Quentin II is another of the Compsons who manages to escape the sick world of her family. His conclusion is that though the primitives are overwhelmed by the presence of the forces of sickness, they are there to bring a modicum of relief. Perhaps, if Backman has included women with his primitives, he would have read the significance of both Caddy and Quentin II's escapes as optimistic. Backman is careful to state that Faulkner's primitivism is not founded on any consistent philosophical base or firm conviction, but functions primarily as an unexamined idealization.[70]

Because he probably expected some disciplined philosophy of primitivism in Faulkner, Cleanth Brooks denies that it is there at all. In fact, he says, "I find little or no primitivism in Faulkner's works."[71] In his strict definition of what primitivism is, Brooks states that Faulkner's persistent use of the child, the idiot, and the Negro cannot or should not be classified as such. Though he does not agree with other critics as to the use of the child, the idiot, and the Negro as primitive norms, he does consider the child, the Negro, and *the woman* important in understanding Faulkner's purposes. In regard to woman, he states: "She can be rather than do. Her loyalties are more immediate and concrete than those of men; her instincts are more fundamental. She is closer to nature.... It is here, I think, that those who claim that Faulkner is a primitivist could ...come closest to making out a case."[72] Brooks, however, does not dwell on this possibility since his thesis is that there is no primitivism in Faulkner.

Howe's study of Faulkner notes the cultural primitivism, the longing for wilderness, the feeling that "wilderness is primal, source and scene of mobility and freedom, innocence; society after it appears, begins to suffocate these values."[73] However, in contrast to Brooks, Howe sees woman not as part of nature, but as the agent of its violation. He catalogues all the negative characterizations of Faulkner's female characters, excepting the splendid old ladies, and concludes: "Women are the this-worldly sex, the childbearers who chain men to possessions and embody the indestructible urge to racial survival. As the personification of the reality principle, they contrive to perpetuate the species no matter what dreams or destruction men indulge in."[74] Howe does not see the positive implications of this view of women nor the connection between this attitude and Faulkner's primitivism. That Faulkner's revulsion at women's "periodic filth" or "womanflesh" should coexist with his admiration for female fortitude is in keeping with his concept of woman as *other,* his acceptance of the myth of the mystery of womanhood.

The introduction to Volpe's *A Reader's Guide to William Faulkner* affirms Faulkner's use of the primitive man as a character type set up as an antithesis to the imprisoned, alienated, confused, and fragmented social man. Volpe sees the primitives as people who "do not resist the conditions in which they find themselves, but accept them and make the best adjustments they can. They are open to experience; they are spontaneous and natural. Because humans are part of the natural world, natural and unconditioned responses are in harmony with nature."[75] Though Volpe includes women, Negroes, and Indians among Faulkner's primitives, he does not develop the idea. He does point out that Faulkner's vision of nature was not idealistic. Faulkner knew that the pattern of existence is brutal; the life-death cycle, the spring and the winter of the earth are reality in Faulkner's world.[76]

Vickery is another of those critics who have noticed the connection between Faulkner's women and his Negroes: "In one sense, the Negroes bear the same relation to the plantation system as the women do to the clan. They are at the very basis of its structure, and, like the women, they have no individual identity."[77] Vickery describes Faulkner's primitivism though she does not call it that. She explains that in Faulkner's value system, the pressures of society would be too much if it were not that the land itself taught man virtue and lent him strength.

> What it teaches is a sense of perspective and hence of values. In the land's persistence throughout all changes, man sees that those values which are most truly his are themselves eternal... that violence and destruction and even death become fully significant only when seen over against the larger rhythms of birth and renewal that order the natural world.[78]

Though she senses Faulkner's primitivism, she does not name it, and though she makes the connection between woman and Negro, Vickery does not make the concurrent identification of women and Negroes as primitives who are in tune with the larger rhythms of the natural cycle.

Collins provides many clues that help establish the connections between Faulkner's attitude toward the indestructibility of women and his characterization of them. In a study of the links between Nathanael West's *The Day of the Locust* and *Sanctuary*, Collins makes the claim that West showed his admiration for Faulkner's work by the "skillful (and entirely proper) use he made of *Sanctuary* while writing *The Day of the Locust*."[79] The parallels that Collins explores do not include a comparison of Faye Greener and Temple Drake in terms of their indestructibility. However, that similarity is remarkable. In West's novel Faye Greener is characterized in this way: "Nothing could hurt her. She was like a cork. No matter how rough the sea got, she would go dancing over the same waves that sank iron ships and tore away piers of reinforced concrete."[80] The image of Faye as a cork is obviously meant to convey a sense of her indestructible character. Collins's failure to note the similarity between Faye and Temple in this context is interesting because in an earlier article about *Sanctuary* he asserts that Faulkner had told a friend that the novel was partly written to show that women can survive almost anything.[81] According to Collins, Faulkner had heard the core of what became Temple and Popeye's story from a woman identified only as N. N's story, even more horrible than the one Faulkner tells, created in Faulkner a sense of "awe for the real counterpart of Temple Drake." Yet, Collins, in his article two years later about West's and Faulkner's stories, only recognizes the redemptive message in the characterization of Ruby Lamar. He concludes that though *Sanctuary* is usually regarded as a book of almost total despair, *Locust* is more depressing because West did not include in his novel "any character so admirable as the dignified, stoical, realistic Ruby Lamar, who gives to *Sanctuary* a tragic air above shock and corncob scandal."[82]

Because of Faulkner's ability to make otherwise unappealing characters his representatives of forbearance and endurance, readers have often missed the optimistic message of their being. The traditional personifications of hope are good, beautiful, bright, or otherwise appealing. Faulkner's prevailing characters can run the gamut from questionable virtue to slowness of wit. This, along with Faulkner's feelings of combined attraction and revulsion toward them, complicates interpretation. The result has been what one might call the small industry of Faulkner criticism, in which each new critical insight adds to rather than vanquishes previous interpretations, for Faulkner's characterizations are so complex as to offer themselves up like so many impressionistic paintings. Each daub of paint contributes to the general image, but viewed separately or too closely to the exclusion of the other daubs, means little.

Thus one writer identifies this or that attitude or type of character and while a few readings are so off the mark as to be entirely discountable, many interpretations leave one assenting, as Faulkner did, to variant readings of his works: "That's possible. Of course, I didn't think of that at the time... but that's possible, that's valid."[83] Thus the identification of the indestructible woman as a type, heretofore not identified in precisely these terms, has been partially suggested by a number of other readers though not in such a manner as to present the total image. Those who come closest are the critics who identify the importance of earth mother characters in Faulkner.[84]

Ambiguities in Faulkner's presentation of women have interfered with piecing together much of the evidence that builds a case for the redemptive paradigm of the indestructible woman.[85] Obvious distaste for or repugnance toward "womanflesh" or "womanfilth" is expressed by many of Faulkner's male characters. His own difficulties in coming to terms with sexually mature women are not only suggested by his behavior toward Meta Carpenter but also in his subsequent affairs with Joan Williams, young enough to be his daughter, and Jean Stein, who was also much younger than he.[86] Still, everything we know about Faulkner's attitude toward the human condition as well as his sense of the prevailing verities suggests that he was not limited in his vision of who or what could bring about redemption. *Requiem for a Nun* is an object lesson that for Faulkner saviors could be personified by black, ex-junkie prostitutes, and even a Temple Drake could be progenitor for the future. His repulsion, nay in fact his horror, would not stop him from presenting even women toward whom he felt revulsion as paradigms for perseverance.

Even the repugnance toward the matter which is woman is in keeping with the mixture of awe and horror that characterizes the worship of such mother goddesses as Kali, who holds a rice bowl in one hand and a knife in the other. Woman is Mother, is Mater, is Matter, is Materies, and insomuch as she is matter, she, like all matter, is subject to decay. "For men, there has often seemed to be something excessively physical about women—too many secretions."[87] There is an instinctive recoil from these mysterious secretions, birth fluids, menstruation. The recoil, however, does not preclude the awe.

Moreover, the decay is necessary for the redemption. It is expressed explicitly in the Eleusinian mysteries that grew out of the Demeter/Persephone mythic pattern. In the rites of Eleusis, Demeter receives a gravid sow as a sacrifice. The pig and the grain are symbolic parallels; both are plowed into the earth. Both are connected with corruption. Grain decays under the earth and in the state of this fruitful death symbolizes the Kore dwelling in the realm of the dead.[88] It is an easy step to an analogy between the grain decaying to bring forth fruit and the woman menstruating in order to signal fecundity. Decay and fertility are two parts of the same whole. Inherent in birth is the inevitability of death; engendering dooms one to death. Mother Earth eventually engulfs the bones of her children. Romantic primitivism might see nature as benign, but Faulkner's is an antiromantic primitivism tinged with a strong sense of irony. His perpetuators of the species can be corrupt, dissimulate, be active or passive; their value is in their fortitude and commitment to continuity.

It is apparent that the indestructible female as she appears in the works of William Faulkner is not the result of a simple conscious effort. The connection of woman to earth, as Mother Earth or Mother Nature, is as ancient as history, a history written by men.[89] Faulkner's women are seen only through the possibilities reflected in this patriarchal view. That this female, as she appears in Faulkner, has been criticized as less than human, malevolent or abhorrent, is in keeping with her mythological construct. Studies of the Great Mother archetype have been undertaken not only by archaeologists and historians, but more recently by psychologists such as Erich Neumann, Carl Jung, Wolfgang Lederer, and M. Esther Harding, who have paid special attention to the problem of her significance because of its implications for the future of therapy in our society. In the introduction to his study of *The Great Mother: An Analysis of the Archetype,* Neumann points out the necessity for understanding how the archetype has worked in our culture: "Western mankind must arrive at a synthesis that includes the feminine world—which is also one-sided in its isolation. Only then will the individual human beings be able to develop the psychic wholeness that is urgently needed if Western Man is to face the dangers that threaten his existence from within and without."[90]

Since the Faulknerian world of Yoknapatawpha County is obviously not one of psychic wholeness, one would hardly expect to find woman there representative of such a view. Faulkner's characters, especially the males, are psychologically troubled individuals who operate in a "border-line" and "bud-like" mythic overstructure. Though Faulkner's world is inhabited by men, women and children, blacks and whites, aristocrats and poor whites, the prevailing perception is that of the white male. The problems of dealing with the past, with race, with the "slings and arrows of outrageous fortune" seem essentially his. Other types may be part of his problem or may have already come to terms with life and thereby serve as models. Women play a significant role in the mythic overstructure that the men are trying to cope with, but large as that role might be it is generally presented by a subjective viewer. Often the parts women play in these tales of sound and fury are primarily assigned on the basis of what Faulkner perceived to be an essential characteristic of their womanhood, their ability to endure and prevail, their indestructibility.

3

Hemingway

Hemingway and Faulkner were very much aware of each other as they made their marks in the American literary landscape. From a distance they metaphorically circled each other like two bucks, occasionally feinting, alternately praising and questioning each other's abilities. Though Faulkner was older by a few years, Hemingway's reputation and international readership were established earlier. Then Faulkner's critical reputation grew steadily as Hemingway's was being reevaluated. Faulkner won the 1949 Nobel Prize; Hemingway was not accorded the same honor until 1954. There were similarities in their personal histories. Both had wanted to be in the service of their country for World War I; both had had to make do with alternatives. Hemingway was wounded in Italy while Faulkner hurt himself in an aerial escapade in Canada. After the war they were both encouraged and helped by Sherwood Anderson; they both repaid Anderson's kindness with ungrateful satire. Hemingway joined the expatriate crowd in Paris. Much of his fiction is set in Europe. Faulkner's European sojourn was briefer and less remarkable. The most significant use of a European setting in his fiction is the one brief scene at the end of *Sanctuary* when Temple Drake blankly looks out at the Luxembourg Gardens.

There are undeniable similarities between these two giants of their time, one of which may be responsible for an attitude they shared about women's indomitability. Both were raised in households where the matriarch reigned. Both of their mothers were strong, independent, and artistic women, married to men with whom they were not particularly compatible, men who were less assertive than they were. Grace Hall Hemingway was first an opera singer and then became a painter; Maud Butler Falkner's paintings hang in many of the rooms at Rowan Oak. Both Faulkner and Hemingway were introduced early to the allures of the woods, learning as boys to hunt and to fish, developing a passion for these activities which they carried into adulthood. For both of these men the outdoors served as a masculine refuge, a place of bonding with other men, away from the strong female presence of hearth and home.

Undeniably, they both had in their lives strong female role models upon which to base a sense of womanly indomitability, but, though there are some similarities in the characterization of indestructible women in the works of Faulkner and Hemingway, there are so many differences in the literary framework within which each author presents his "truth" that a different set of premises must be established in order to effectively examine the indomitable or enduring qualities of woman as she is presented in the works of Ernest Hemingway.

A salient difference in their literary frameworks is in the type of perceptor each author uses. Faulkner is one of the great experimenters with point of view. His narrators are mostly men, but sometimes women and children. Part of the effectiveness of his vision is achieved by his layering of perceptions. Once he had discovered his mythic "kingdom," the telling of its story, the coming to terms with its past, present, and future, was his continuing task. The corpus of his works shows us a land and its people, rich and poor, young and old, black and white. His Yoknapatawpha cycle is the story of their history, social readjustments, and interactions as they struggle with the onerous past, difficult present, and doubtful future. His protagonists, though predominantly white male, represent a multiplicity of racial, sexual, social, and chronological frames of reference.

Hemingway's narrative technique is quite different. Almost all of his short stories and novels are seen through the perception of a single narrator, invariably male. Whereas in Faulkner the settings are limited to a specific region in the South while the narrators vary, in Hemingway the settings are dispersed across three continents while the invariable masculine viewpoint persists. Even when there is the rare female protagonist, such as in the early short stories "Up in Michigan" and "Cat in the Rain," the story is still told by the omniscient or distanced narrator. Two female viewpoints are presented in *To Have and Have Not*, but their scope is miniscule in comparison to the male viewpoints that predominate.

Not only are Hemingway's protagonists and perceptors predominantly male, but they operate in a specialized male environment. There are no equivalents for the Compson children, Chick Mallison, or Bayard and Ringo in Hemingway's world. His youngest protagonist is Nick Adams, and Nick is a child in only a few of the short stories. When Nick Adams's familial situation is presented in the short stories, it is for the purpose of exploring its effect on him, the individual protagonist, not of turning attention to parent/child relationships or sibling rivalry. Except in a few short stories, Hemingway does not choose to depict the everyday, the mundane, the multiple possibilities of different individuals acting, reacting, and interacting. The protagonists of his novels operate in supercharged, romantic environments: the confrontation with death, war, corridas, safari, fishing trips, male-dominated worlds.

Women, when they enter these worlds, are usually alone. In fact, there is a scarcity of female characters in all of Hemingway's novels.

While there is no discernable character who is prominent enough in Faulkner's works to be designated "the Faulkner hero"—in fact much of Faulkner scholarship centers on trying to discern just which of his characters speaks for him—the "Hemingway hero" is practically a cliche; even people who haven't read Hemingway know what is meant by a Hemingway hero. Faulkner narrates his fiction through the perception of the villainous and the virtuous, the intelligent and the mentally deficient, the sane and the mad. His protagonists, when they are not his narrators, are equally varied. Hemingway's novels, without exception, detail the experiences of a male protagonist whose age approximates Hemingway's at the time he is writing the work. Hemingway's early heroes are Jake Barnes and Frederick Henry, young men trying to cope with World War I and its aftereffects. His last heroes are Colonel Cantwell and Santiago, grizzled veterans of life's battles and struggles, remembering past pains and triumphs, trying to transmit their knowledge to the younger generation.[1]

Along with his invariable male protagonist, Hemingway's plot patterns are remarkably repetitive. Whether it be in darkest Africa, war-torn Italy, the Caribbean, or the bullring, the Hemingway plot replicates the archetypal quest. According to their ages and situations, Hemingway's heroes follow certain ritualistic patterns in their search for initiation and meaning. Young Nick Adams tries to make sense out of life as he copes with his experiences and goes through the rites of hunting and fishing in the North Woods. Jake Barnes, in his solitary anguish, searches for a way to live his wounded existence: "All I wanted to know was how to live in it" (SAR, 118). Francis Macomber uses the rite of the hunt to try to recover his lost manhood, which as Wilson points out is not a matter of being 21, but of dealing with fear. Harry in "The Snows of Kilimanjaro" is searching for a return of meaning to his life. He goes to Africa "to start again" (SSOEH, 59). Robert Jordan tries to give his life and death meaning through devotion to a cause. Colonel Cantwell returns to scenes of military exploits to try to regain a sense of his life before he dies. Santiago journeys to the uncharted waters of the Caribbean to prove that though man can be destroyed, he cannot be defeated.

The pattern is pervasive. The terrain may vary, the form of the rite may change, the hero ages, but the quest pattern prevails. The hero goes through a testing of self, facing the existential question of how to live or how to die. The focus is singularly masculine as the man goes through his testing ritual. This focus is reinforced in each story's conclusion because the end of each novel finds the hero either alone or dead.[1] Cantwell dies alone. Frederick Henry is left alone when Catherine dies. Robert Jordan dies alone defending the retreat of Maria and the others. Harry, of "The Snows of Kilimanjaro," dies essentially alone as he has alienated himself from his wife. Francis Macomber is killed after a "short" life as a man. Harry Morgan goes through his death ordeal alone. Jake Barnes is left very much alone, having prostituted his *afición*, without even his illusions to sustain him. Obviously, man alone is the subject of Hemingway's works. The male character, as he plots his quest, is well defined and well developed. This is not true for the women characters in Hemingway.[2]

Critics complain about the malevolence of Faulkner's characterization of women. But Hemingway is condemned not only for the malevolence of his characterizations, but also for his shallow and superficial portrayals of female characters.[3] A major complaint is that he uses his female characters as devices, "a convenience, and a technique to turn a monologue into a dialogue."[4] The shallow or superficial portrayal is usually blamed on Hemingway's narrow concept of masculinity, the subject of much critical derision. The Hemingway hero attempts to drink well, shoot well, throw the straight and true punch, prove his proficiency and potency in intercourse, and when his time comes, die heroically. The Hemingway philosophy or code from which this behavior results has been called "adolescent," "ego run riot," "machismo," and "male-ism." Whatever its appellation, this kind of orientation, exclusively male, tends to place the woman at one of two opposing poles. Definitely *other,* object not subject, she is reduced to playing the role of functionary in man's fulfillment. If she performs in a reinforcing way, she is a positive functionary. In this role she is pliant and submissive, sometimes helpful. She does not interfere with his quest and is often the tool through which he wins his merit badge for sexual potency. In her negative function the woman is knowingly and unknowingly threatening and destructive. She distracts or otherwise keeps the hero from his goal.

Both boosters and detractors have noted that Hemingway's female characters tend to fall into two distinct categories. Those who consider this an artistic failure point out that most real women occupy a middle ground between the two extremes. Edmund Wilson claims that Hemingway's docile and pliant females are like projections of youthful erotic dreams, not real at all.[5] Leslie Fiedler goes a step further. He says, "There are no *women* in Hemingway."[6] Katherine Rogers takes a middle position. She says that his "good" women are creations of erotic fantasy, while his realistically depicted women are destructive. She attributes this stylization to a fear which expressed itself through a preference for undemanding primitives.[7] Fiedler and Wilson also conclude that Hemingway's failure in the area of female characterization is a result of fear. Fiedler's contention is that the fear signified a rejection of sexual maturity, while Wilson says that Hemingway ascribes to the theory that "the female is deadlier than the male." The source of Hemingway's fear of women, according to John W. Presley, is the medieval idea that a man has only so much vital fluid and that intercourse with women drains his psychic and sexual energy reserves.[8] Carol H. Smith notes that Hemingway attributes the destruction of Eden and the failure of romantic love to women, thereby exonerating himself from responsibility for the failure of his romantic relationships; this he does partially because of his fear of his own susceptibility to romantic love and partially out of his equally strong fear of being dominated by women.[9]

The element of fear is also significant in Faulkner's ambivalent characterization of the female.[10] The nature of that fear, however, is quite different from the fear projected in Hemingway's characterizations. Faulkner's fear is couched in terms which evoke images of the overwhelming power of female sexuality: Eula's body is described as "too much mammalian female meat" or "the supreme primal uterus"; Belle's effect is likened to drowning in a "motionless and cloying sea." For Faulkner women's unbridled sexuality precludes chastity. Women are never virgins, Mr. Compson tells Quentin, because virginity is a negative state and therefore contrary to nature. The mistrust of women projected in Faulkner's works is identified with their fecundity. His earth mother types are often anonymously and promiscuously pregnant; the paternity is frequently uncertain. Gail Hightower, whose opinion is independent of his individual situation and can therefore be given added weight in this context, states, "No woman who has a child is ever betrayed; the husband of a mother, whether he be a father or not, is already a cuckold" (LIA, 298–99). The number of men in Faulkner who act as fathers to children that are not biologically theirs is significant.[11] The suggestion is that the very productivity of the female is designed to cheat the male.

The fear of cuckoldry, while unsettling, is mild when compared to the anxieties that underlie the fear of women projected in Hemingway's works. What man has to fear in Hemingway is his very being and most especially his manhood, his *cojones*. The danger begins early. Hemingway's attitude toward mothers, illustrated in his characterization of Mrs. Adams, Nick's mother, and also of other of his motherlike women who treat their men like boys, may have preceded Philip Wylie's hysterical diatribe against "momism," but it seems a perfect illustration of it. Wylie developed his theory of "momism" to describe what he saw as the preponderance of American women who were dominating their men; he saw American women as emasculating, neurotic, and pampered creatures, who would not allow their male children to reach maturity.[12] Such women are dangerous, not because they may betray a man, but because they will not allow him to be a man.[13] If the woman's goal, conscious or unconscious, is complete domination, then only a completely subservient female will not be threatening.

Though they do not deny the superficiality of Hemingway's rendering of the female character, sympathetic critics such as Carlos Baker justify it on the grounds that it is a merger of style and theme. Hemingway's famous style pares things down to essentials, and since Hemingway's novels and short stories are really about man alone, woman is only relevant in a functionary capacity.[14] She acts as a modus operandi in the service of his art, performing a symbolic or ritualistic function in the quest for meaning in the hero's life. As such, Hemingway's females are much like the mythological goddesses or sorceresses the hero encounters in the archetypal quest or journey in classical mythology.

One of the main features of the hero cycle is ritual testing to prove worthiness.[15] In mythology the testing is oftimes of a physical nature, sometimes mental, and can involve a journey. Examples that come easily to mind are Jason's search for the golden fleece, Theseus's testing in the labyrinth and against the minotaur, Oedipus and the Sphinx, Ulysses's many voyages. Translated to Hemingway's work, the testing becomes a baptism of fire in war, facing the wounded lion in Africa, fighting the brave bull in Spain, or fending off sharks in the waters of Cuba. In the mythological stories, the hero encounters goddesses or sorceresses who either aid him or deter him or do both. Medea helps Jason secure the golden fleece and get away from her father and brothers though she destroys him later; Ariadne aids Theseus and is, in turn, deserted by him; Circe turns Ulysses's men into swine, though she later marries Ulysses; the Sphinx holds the key to both Oedipus's victory and tragedy.

Though the relegation of Hemingway's female characters to the ranks of either destructive or helpful goddesses—bitch-goddesses or corn-goddesses—is tempting and follows the line of much thoughtful and discerning criticism, stopping at that interpretive level overlooks a deeper and more basic significance of the woman as portrayed in Hemingway. Erich Neumann has explained that the hero cycle is a projection of the pattern of the maturation cycle of the individual consciousness. Read in that way Hemingway's heroes, as they go through their cycles, can be interpreted as representatives of steps in their creator's psychic development. The impetus for making this kind of biographical assumption derives not only from the fact that Hemingway's vision is so singularly masculine, but also because his protagonists reflect his age as well as his experience. That his characters are drawn from real models is a fact that is generally accepted. There are books and articles in which the aptness of his portrayals is challenged or verified. Phillip Young's psychobiographical reading of Hemingway's works posits the theory that the personal element in Hemingway's fiction is too strong to ignore and that it results in great part from the trauma caused by his wound in World War I.[16] Scott Donaldson also believes that he can create a mosaic of the Hemingway's mind and personality by looking primarily at his fiction.[17]

Young and Hoffman stress the importance of the actual physical wound and its resultant trauma in explaining the character of Hemingway's protagonists. Illuminating as this might be in helping to understand the behavior of Hemingway's male characters, it does little to solve the puzzle of Hemingway's female characterizations, for many of Hemingway's attitudes toward women were formed much before his wounding. If there is a trauma relevant to those attitudes it stems from the trauma of birth and the subsequent need for the child to establish a self separate from the maternal oneness. Normally a man's initial perception of women is formed by his relationship with his mother. She is his first model of the feminine. In the course of his individual development, the male child must struggle to exchange his identification with the feminine for one with its opposite—the masculine. For every child the struggle for individuation is a difficult one and often results in a negative characterization of that which one must struggle against. In this battle the feminine achieves a dual character—one aspect of which is the Terrible Mother, the opposite of the protecting and nourishing mother. According to Jungian psychologists, each child retains primordial images of both mothers in the subconscious. Hemingway's depiction of women follows the pattern of the primordial archetype of the Great Mother, an archetype which embodies both of these extremes: "It is an essential feature of the primordial archetype that it combines positive and negative attributes and groups of attributes. This union of opposites...ambivalence, is characteristic of the original situation of the unconscious, which consciousness has not yet dissected into its antithesis."[18]

These coexisting elements of the archetypal mother account for such things as the paradoxical earth symbolism which can see the womb of the earth, in one instance generative and nourishing, become the deadly devouring maw of the Underworld. The nourishing and protecting womb becomes the devouring womb of the grave and of death, of darkness without light. In the archetypal symbolism of things Mother Earth who generates life and all things on earth is the same Mother Earth who takes all things back into herself, the hungry earth who devours her own children.[19] In a profound way, life and birth are inextricably bound with death and destruction. The extreme characterizations of most of Hemingway's female creations evidence the reality of this paradoxical situation. They either nurture or they destroy, and sometimes do both.

Information about Hemingway's interactions with three of the most significant women in his early life, women who helped to form his attitudes toward the opposite sex, provides a basis for understanding the character of many of his female creations. Subsequent relationships did not have the same impact either on his character or on his art. The women who most influenced him were his mother, Grace Hall Hemingway; the woman he first proposed to, Agnes von Kurowsky; and his first wife, Hadley Richardson, the mother of his first son.[20] These women provided the archetypes, the primal patterns against which other women were measured. All three were older than he was; all three treated him in a maternal manner; all three exemplified aspects of the positive and negative features of the Great Mother. But more than that, all three were enduring types who functioned very well without him, maintained their selfhood, indomitable survivors. Harry Levin has pointed out that though much of Hemingway's work professes an attitude of near-nihilistic despair, there are certain abilities that excite his admiration. "The good fight of the lost cause" and the capacity to endure punishment, a "stoic or masochistic determination to take it," are two of the positive qualities he admires.[21] These women, and by extension the characters modeled after them, display these indomitable characteristics.

The first indomitable woman in Hemingway's life was his mother. From all accounts, Grace Hall Hemingway was a remarkable person. She had six children and maintained a career teaching music; she had given up the possibility of becoming an opera singer in order to marry. However, she was not interested in housekeeping or in occupying herself with other traditional housewifely activities such as cooking or sewing. And she earned enough money to see to it that she did not have to.[22] In a time before such terminology was in vogue, she wanted her own "space" and, with her own money, saw to it that a small cabin, christened "Gracie's house," was built for her so that she could get away from the demands of family and be alone.[23] She was active in the Suffragette movement, dragging the child Ernest along to meetings. At the age of 52 she launched a new career as a landscape painter. The woman was anything but pliant and docile.

There was between Ernest and his mother the normal tension that naturally results from a boy having to mature and assert himself. The normal stress and strain was added to by the fact that Dr. and Mrs. Hemingway had quite opposite interests. Grace Hemingway tried to push her son in the direction of her musical inclinations, while Clarence "Ed" Hemingway encouraged his boy's interest in hunting and fishing. In discussions about their individual parents, as well as in discussions about the senior Hemingways' marriage, the family divides along lines of sex. Ernest and his brother Leicester criticized their mother's lack of interest in housework, deplored her "selfish" desire to be alone, and rejected her need to assert her independence and creativity. Their reactions are predictably sexist. The Hemingway daughters and many friends outside the family are not as critical. They remember Grace Hemingway as a warm, vibrant woman who always took center stage when she entered a room. At least one Hemingway sister has suggested that competition for that center of attention may have been at the heart of Ernest's problems with his mother.

Both Dr. and Mrs. Hemingway had strong feelings about the work ethic and when Ernest returned from his time overseas and showed little inclination to support himself, they were worried about what they perceived as his lack of purpose. Grace Hemingway was also hurt by his thoughtlessness toward her, indicating in a letter which called him to task for taking much more than he was giving, that an interest in hearing her sing, or tell stories, or play the piano might earn him some credit in her book.[24]

After an episode of particular pain and embarrassment to Mrs. Hemingway, a secret midnight picnic, she handed Ernest a letter which chastised him for being lazy, loafing, and pleasure-seeking. She accused him of trading on his handsome face and trying to "graft a living off of anybody and everybody." She told him that the world needed men—real men with both moral and physical brawn and muscle—and extolled the virtues of the man he was named for, her father. She told him that when he had changed his ideas and aims in life, he would find his mother waiting to welcome him, in this world or in the next. She assured him that she loved him and desired his love in return. Her signature indicated that she was still hoping and praying for his reformation.[25] Ernest never forgave her. Leicester Hemingway described the letter as formally drumming Ernest out of the family. "Few affronts to personal dignity could top that of holding a ceremonial dinner on a twenty-first birthday while getting ready to slip the guest of honor a letter asking him to kindly leave the premises."[26] In Ernest's perception the assertion of his manhood had resulted in rejection by his mother. One of the main points of her letter was that he had changed so much since he was "her dear little boy."[27]

Grace Hemingway held strong views about proper behavior and her attitudes remained unchanged even after Ernest had won national recognition for his writing. She disapproved of his choice of language and subject matter and did not hesitate to make her feeling known to her son. He responded in a letter which told her that "he felt that Dad had been very loyal while Mother had not been loyal at all."[28] Hemingway's hostility toward his mother lasted the whole of his and her lifetimes; she lived to be 79. When she was a 77-year-old woman, ailing and in need of nursing care, he was reduced to threatening her to keep her from giving interviews about him. He called her, to various interviewers, a domineering shrew and an all-time, all-American bitch. The first big psychic wound he suffered, said Hemingway, was a result of finding out that his father was a coward.[29] He blamed his mother for driving his father to suicide. Early critics seemed willing to accept Hemingway's portrayal, especially as it was supported by Leicester. More recent studies and interviews with the Hemingway daughters present a more balanced perspective. A recent essay by Max Westbrook was written specifically to correct what he feels is an "inaccurate and unfair" characterization of Grace, particularly in regard to her handling of the situation in the summer of 1920.[30]

Many of Hemingway's indestructible bitches or terrible mothers are projections of his negative feelings about his own mother. The most obvious example is Mrs. Adams, Nick's mother, who is, among other things, like Grace Hemingway a doctor's wife. The autobiographical aspect of the Adams family is undeniable. As portrayed by Hemingway, American women are often indomitable but deadly, dangerous to men. If they do not drive their husbands to suicide literally, they destroy them spiritually. Sometimes it is their very strength that a man cannot match that undermines him.

Nick Adams, one of Hemingway's earliest autobiographical protagonists, learns about women's strength as he watches his mother dominate his father. But Mrs. Adams is not the only example of female ascendancy Nick encounters while growing up. In the short story "Indian Camp" Nick watches his father perform a cesarean section on an Indian woman without even an anesthetic to alleviate her pain. The Indian woman, whose body bears the pain, survives, but her husband, who has been listening to her ordeal, kills himself. The climactic conversation in the story takes place between Dr. Adams and his son:

> "Why did he kill himself, Daddy?"
> "He couldn't stand things, I guess."
> "Do many men kill themselves, Daddy?"
> "Not very many, Nick."
> "Do many women?"
> "Hardly ever." (SSOEH, 95)

The implication is that men are somehow not able to tolerate the agonies of life. Men can't stand things. Women can. The Indian woman survives labor for two days and then a primitive operation without benefit of anesthetic. Dr. Adams performs the operation with a jackknife and sews up the incision with nine-foot, tapered gut leaders. Indeed, the actual physical pain that the Indian woman would have to go through is not even considered by Dr. Adams. He does not bother to bring the proper equipment with him when he is summoned to the woman's aid. Dr. Adams's behavior is racist as well as sexist; surely he would not go to an Anglo woman's bedside so ill prepared. This insensitivity and carelessness is not highlighted by Hemingway; in fact, it seems irrelevant to the point except for those readers who might consider the woman's point of view. The only rationale for Adams's actions is his attitude that this woman could survive or stand anything, an attitude he communicates to his son.

The second important mother figure in Hemingway's life was Agnes H. von Kurowsky, the nurse he fell "wildly" in love with when he was wounded in Italy. She was his first adult love affair and he wanted very much to marry her. Agnes, however, was some seven years older than Ernest and she was not ready to commit herself to marriage. She took care of him when he was wounded and encouraged him to return home, promising to follow him. One of the reasons that she wanted him to return home was her fear of his turning into a "sponger." Ernest had been offered the opportunity to live and travel in Europe, with no responsibilities except having fun, all expenses paid. Like Grace Hemingway, Agnes von Kurowsky was concerned about Ernest's penchant for taking. Agnes feared he would turn into a bum.[31] Because she was older, she tried to direct him on the right path, in effect, to mother him.

Agnes's affection for Ernest was genuine, but she was by her own account quite fickle. When she left New York for Italy, she was unofficially engaged to a doctor in America. Shortly after Ernest left Italy she became involved with a new lover, Tenente Dominico Carracciolo, of the Italian nobility. Though her letters of the period are quite loving, Agnes was not ready to return to the States and settle down. She liked the life she was leading, enjoyed her nursing, and did not want to give up her career.[32]

The difference in their ages was underlined by the fact that she called him "the Kid." There is general agreement that the relationship was never sexually consummated except in Hemingway's imagination. Agnes's fictional counterpart, Catherine Barkley, begging Frederick not to leave her ("You won't go away?") is a clear projection of what Hemingway wishes Agnes had said. But she did not. She wanted him safely back in America.

When Agnes finally wrote to tell him that she was in love with someone else, Hemingway was devastated. His brother Leicester remembers that "her refusal hit Ernest like a second mortar shell, and he reacted violently...."[33] He was dismayed and horrified by her rejection. The reaction was so severe that he began to run a temperature and had to go to bed. He raged against her and his rage took the form of a desire for revenge.[34] Later, he worked these feelings out in several short stories as well as in the characters of Catherine Barkley whom he kills off and Brett Ashley, a nurse who is denied the man she loves.[35] Agnes, however, was made of sterner stuff than her fictional representations. Taking her unfortunate love affair in stride, she left Italy a "sadder but wiser girl," to lead a very adventurous life working and traveling in such places as Paris, Bucharest, Constantinople, Athens, and Naples. She found out about the publication of *A Farewell to Arms* when she was director of nurses, working at the Haitian General Hospital. She was big-hearted and independent enough to respond to a letter from Ernest (taking his letter as a sign that he had overcome his bitterness toward her) by saying that she was proud of him and wished him well. "I always knew that it would turn out right in the end," she reassured him.[36]

The wound of Agnes's rejection was soothed first by Hadley and then by success. Like Agnes, Hadley was older than Ernest. In fact, there was about the same difference in their ages. Whereas Agnes had a career to make her self-sufficient, Hadley had a small inheritance. Unlike Agnes, Hadley was willing to use the whole of her resources to sustain and support Ernest. Ernest's nonfictional depiction of her, three wives later, is of an ever thoughtful, always supportive, mothering woman. Her unselfish love for him was so strong that, once she was certain that their marriage was over, she made divorcing her as easy as possible. She was neither hostile, remonstrative, nor bitter. In the letter that she wrote to him agreeing to his initiation of the divorce proceedings, she was still mothering him. Eat well, she cautioned him; sleep well, keep well, and work well. The letter is signed, "with Mummy's love."[37] Hadley's supportive behavior did not end with their divorce; she continued to act as surrogate mother all the rest of his life. In the years that followed, he wrote her letters complaining of his treatment by his subsequent wives. Like Agnes, Hadley got on quite well without Ernest. She recovered from the trauma of the divorce and showed remarkable resiliency and adaptability. She remarried and lived happily with her second husband, Paul Mowrer, a Pulitzer Prize-winning foreign correspondent. In Hemingway's perception she was ever brave, true, unselfish, lovely, and generous even at the time of their divorce.[38] With the passage of time, his opinion of her never wavered.

His feelings of guilt about his betrayal of her were never assuaged.[39] Three marriages followed. None of his subsequent wives appears as blameless as Hadley either in his fictional or nonfictional depiction of them. In *A Moveable Feast*, written while he was married to his fourth wife Mary, he says that he wishes he had died before he ever loved a woman other than Hadley (MF, 208). The relationship with Hadley set the pattern for his depiction of submissive and beneficial women. Such women as Maria in *For Whom the Bell Tolls*, Catherine Barkley in *A Farewell to Arms*, and Renata in *Across the River and into the Trees* all speak in a manner suggestive of a mother talking to a child in grammar school-level language. Hadley's dialogue as represented by Hemingway in *A Moveable Feast* has much the same tone.

Hemingway's indestructible women characters, then, are projections of his responses to the three main women in his life during the years when his understanding of the female sex was being formed. Like his mother and Agnes and Hadley they have an inner strength, an ability to cope with whatever life dishes out for them. As these three women "mothered" Ernest, so his indestructible women characters often "mother" their men. On the most elementary level they represent the various characteristics, positive and negative, of the Great Mother, an aspect of the archetypal feminine. Hemingway himself appears to have been conscious of these Jungian notions, acknowledging on one occasion that he "believed imagination could be the result of inherited racial experience."[40]

As the Great Mother contains within herself aspects both positive and negative, so Hemingway's "mothering" women function on the archetypal level as either helpful or destructive goddesses. If they are destructive they are representative of the Terrible Mother, the death-giving aspect of the archetypal feminine. If they are docile or submissive, they are aspects of the nourishing mother, the earth or corn goddesses who symbolize the productive capacities of the earth. In their negative aspects they reject and undermine the hero. In their positive function, they mirror him and represent his immortality. While the hero, who is subject, plays out his brief but hectic scene, the woman, who is object, remains like an eternal backdrop, one of the indestructible verities against which man must test his values.[41]

The primary terrible mothers in Hemingway's works are Brett Ashley, Margot Macomber, and Helen in "Snows of Kilimanjaro." They occupy a category I will call the "destructive indestructibles." While they themselves are indomitable and enduring, association with them proves destructive for the men in their lives, a destruction which is not necessarily the woman's fault. One important attribute they all share is physical attractiveness. Like any number of mythical bitch-goddesses or sorceresses such as Circe, the Sirens, or even Aphrodite in her sinister mode, their beauty is one of their lures. Aphrodite in other incarnations was Astarte or Ashtoreth, the goddess of carnal and earthly love. Her allurements are sensual rather than spiritual and Hemingway's bitch-goddesses rule by sensual sway. Their devotees serve them as Aphrodite and Ashtoreth were sometimes served, by religious prostitution. Sometimes this took the form of giving oneself to a stranger in order to serve the goddess. Sometimes the goddess is portrayed in bisexual imagery, imagery used by Hemingway in his characterization of both his nourishing and his destructive women.

Lady Brett Ashley is perhaps one of Hemingway's most attractive destructive women. Her androgynous appearance heightens rather than detracts from her sex appeal.[42] Though she wears her hair like a man's, her figure is described as having "curves like the hull of a racing yacht," and as Jake Barnes notes, she accentuates those curves by wearing wool jersey (SAR, 22). She does not want to adopt a traditionally feminine hairdo and remarks cryptically to Jake that one of the things wrong with her relationship with Pedro Romero was that he wanted her to grow her hair long. "He wanted me to grow my hair out. Me, with long hair. I'd look so like hell" (SAR, 242). Not only does Brett wear her hair in a boyish bob, but she also dresses in mannish clothing. She wears a "man's felt hat" and "a slipover jersey sweater and a tweed skirt" (SAR, 22). Her bisexual image is also suggested by her first appearance in the novel. She walks into the scene with a group of her homosexual friends. Jake describes them first. They too are wearing jerseys. "With them was Brett. She looked very lovely and she was very much with them" (SAR, 20). The suggestion here is that she is very much part of this group, who are men and yet, in Jake's description, mince and gesture in parodies of femininity, masculine and feminine at the same time. Another of Brett's characteristics which acts to blur sexual distinctions is her habit of calling herself "chap." She calls men chaps—"Hello, you chaps"—and then she calls herself the same in ordering a drink—"I say, give a chap a brandy and soda."

The men in her life serve her in much the same manner as religious prostitutes served Aphrodite. First they worship at her shrine; then they prostitute themselves. Jake expresses his adoration of Brett early in the story, telling her he loves her, begging her to live with him. Afterwards, he acts the pimp for her when he sets her up with Pedro Romero. Robert Cohn calls him just that. What is worse, he corrupts his *afición*; that is to say, he prostitutes his passion in order to serve hers. The price is high. At one time he had been acknowledged as one who possessed true *afición*: "When they saw that I had *afición*, and there was no password, no set questions that could bring it out, rather a sort of oral spiritual examination. . . . At once he [they] forgave me all my friends" (SAR, 132). Jake's clout with Montoya, the high priest of the bull cult, has been strong. When Jake prostitutes his *afición* by introducing Pedro Romero to the kind of woman who will, in the eyes of the *aficionados*, ruin him, Montoya will not even nod at Jake. When Jake leaves the hotel, Montoya does not come near him.

But Jake is not the only supplicant for the goddess's favor; more than one of her acolytes prostitutes himself for her. Robert Cohn, in the tradition of giving oneself to a stranger, offers himself to Brett, who is little more than a stranger to him. Once their weekend at San Sebastian is over, she rejects his attempts to give their relationship any special significance. His slavish devotion to her and doglike worship destroy his pride, earn him the animosity of the group, and leave him nothing. In his own words, "I've been through such hell, Jake. Now everything's gone. Everything" (SAR, 194). The final memento he has to carry away from his encounter with Brett is a sock in the face from Pedro Romero.

Mike Campbell is another of the men who is reduced by his association with Brett while she is affected minimally. Not much can be said for Mike's character to begin with, but it is not enhanced by his association with Brett. At the end of the book he has been "cuckolded" in a sense and left alone and penniless. In fact, he is put in the position of a kept man as Brett puts up most of the money that he gives Montoya to pay their bill in Pamplona. Mike's complete degradation is shown in his final scene with Bill Gorton and Jake Barnes when he commits the unpardonable sin of gambling without money to back his bet. He has spent the last bit of money he has buying drinks and giving extravagant tips to the bartender. His complete lack of character is explored by Bill Gorton as he establishes the fact that Mike not only did not have the money to gamble with, but that he has taken all of Brett's money and still intends to sponge off yet another acquaintance when they drop him off.

Brett's role as a goddess to be worshipped is underscored in the scene with the *riau-riau* dancers. "Brett wanted to dance but they did not want her to. They wanted her as an image to dance around" (SAR, 155). Robert Cohn articulates her fatal attraction for men. " 'He calls her Circe,' Mike said. 'He claims she turns men into swine.' " Figuratively she does just that. She calls Mike a swine for the way he treats Robert Cohn, responding to Jake's defense of Mike by saying, "Yes. But he didn't need to be a swine" (SAR, 181). Cohn's behavior is also swinish, as he follows Brett around, sniveling and squealing.

But Brett is not pure bitch-goddess. Certain aspects of her positive mothering qualities are also stressed. She had been a nurse during the war. She and Jake met in a hospital. She "nurses" Romero after his fistfight with Cohn. Mike Campbell comments about her mothering qualities, "She loves looking after people. That's how we came to go off together. She was looking after me" (SAR, 203). Her mothering role is underscored as she tries to maintain harmony in the group, placating the rivalrous siblings. She chides Mike when he is ugly to Cohn. Her effect on the men is analogous to the effect a strong mother has on her sons. Those who do not exert their independence and kill the domination of the Terrible Mother remain tied to her, thereby abdicating their manhood. Those who are strong, like Romero, who maintain their independence and their principles, are set free. Brett's choice to set Romero free is significant here. She chooses to leave him because she knows she is not good for him. In her depiction of her choice she stresses the difference in their ages. "I'm thirty-four, you know. I'm not going to be one of those bitches that ruins children" (SAR, 243).

But analyzing Brett in terms of bitch-goddess or Terrible Mother does not do justice to her. On one level, she does function in that capacity, but Hemingway has done much more with her character. In his original version of *The Sun Also Rises* Brett is more the heroine than she appears in the book as published.[43] She is a complex woman who has suffered much and endured. Her indestructible qualities are revealed as we become aware of her past. Jake tells Cohn that she had married Lord Ashley during the war: "Her own true love had just kicked off with the dysentery" (SAR, 39). The marriage to Ashley is disastrous. According to Mike Campbell,

Ashley, chap she got the title from, was a sailor, you know. Ninth baronet. When he came home he couldn't sleep in a bed. Always made Brett sleep on the floor. Finally, when he got really bad, he used to tell her he'd kill her. Always slept with a loaded service revolver. Brett used to take the shells out when he'd gone to sleep. She hasn't had an absolutely happy life. Brett. Damned shame, too. She enjoys things so. (SAR, 203)

Besides these two devastating personal relationships, her love affair with Jake is a source of continuing frustration because of his inability to consummate the relationship sexually.

Her personal attractiveness and desirability are not affected by her lifestyle. The men want her regardless of her behavior. Though their self-images are dealt blows by their encounters with Brett, she remains with her illusions intact, her desirability unquestioned, and her worshippers still devoted. After he has pimped for her, corrupted his *afición*, been beat up by Cohn, disillusioned with Mike, Jake still comes the moment she beckons him. He goes to Madrid to bail her out of the hotel where she has sent Pedro Romero away though he had wanted to marry her. She claims that she would have lived with Romero if she hadn't seen that it was bad for him. Though Jake is left with next to nothing, Brett comes away from her relationship with Romero with a sense of satisfaction. Romero had loved her, wanting to marry her to prevent her from ever leaving him, but she has decided for his own good not to stay with him. "I'm not going to be that way. I feel rather good you know. I feel rather set up"(SAR, 243). Brett is able to rationalize to herself; Jake is not. He tries to escape in drink. "Don't get drunk Jake," she said. "You don't have to." Jake answers, "How do you know?" But even getting drunk does not help Jake. In the final scene Brett still retains the unshakable illusion that all of her problems would not have been if only she and Jake could have been married. Her "life lie" is safely entrenched. One has the sense that she will go forward to her next affair or marriage armed with the satisfaction of having decided not to be a bitch and the rationalization that all would have been well if only she could have married Jake. She is undaunted. Jake, however, is not so lucky. He does not even have the illusion of the lost chance with her to sustain him anymore. His final remark in the novel clearly indicates that. When Brett says to him, "Oh, Jake, we could have had such a damned good time together," his yes is qualified with "Isn't it pretty to think so?" The word "pretty" for a man like Jake says it all. Pretty is a woman's word. The notion that all would have been good, if only . . . , is an attractive one, a pretty notion, but it is not sound, not substantial.

Margot Macomber is probably the most devastating of Hemingway's "destructive-indestructibles." Like the goddess Rhea, she demands not only self-mutilation and self-emasculation, but ultimately human sacrifice. Margot's role as Terrible Mother is communicated in several ways. She treats both men in the story like difficult children. She rewards their proper acts and punishes their transgressions. When Francis performs poorly, she removes her hand from his. Wilson's fine performance rates a big kiss. When Francis behaves hostilely about her infidelity with Wilson, Margot admonishes him, "Behave yourself." Oedipal strains are provided as Margot, the Great Mother, beds Wilson, the Great White Hunter, a definite father figure. Wilson takes the role of surrogate father to Francis, teaching him the rites and rituals of the hunt and leading him through his initiation into manhood. When Francis does attain it, Wilson in a typically fatherly fashion is proud of him. He even shares his philosophy of life with Francis, quoting Shakespeare's "a man can die but once; we owe God a death and let it go which way it will he that dies this year is quit for the next"(SSOEH, 32). But before Francis has "come of age" it is Wilson's privilege to bed the Great Mother, a privilege established by his "manly" behavior. Francis, like the unworthy son who has not proved himself, can only whine like a petulant boy, "You promised." The next morning, confronting Wilson, Francis's role as son to Wilson's father is reinforced when Wilson admonishes him, "I'd pull yourself together, *laddybuck* (emphasis mine)" (SSOEH, 24). Wilson's musings about Macomber stress his boylike image: "It's that some of them stay little boys so long, Wilson thought. Sometimes all their lives. Their figures stay boyish when they're fifty. The great American boy-men" (SSOEH, 33).

Francis's situation is reminiscent of Oedipus's before he answers the riddle of the Sphinx. Oedipus must walk on his own two feet like a man in the noon of his years, but in this very confrontation with the Sphinx are the seeds of his doom. Paradoxically, the confrontation is possible only when he has reached manhood and has become strong and clever and able, for it is only then that he can fulfill the prophecy. In the myth, the Sphinx, an aspect of the Terrible Mother, kills herself. Hemingway's terrible mothers are not so easily destroyed. When Francis becomes a man, his Terrible Mother destroys him instead.

Margot as Terrible Mother is unimpressed by her children's acts of derring-do. She reduces their male victories to petty triumphs. In this manner she behaves much as Grace Hemingway had on the occasion of Ernest's literary triumphs. When Ernest's first novel attained fame and was accorded some positive criticism, Grace's comment was that "it seemed to her 'a doubtful honor' to have produced 'one of the filthiest books of the year.'" She did, however, go on to encourage him in a manner that undercut all his achievement: "'I love you dear,' wrote Grace, 'and still believe you will do something worthwhile.'"[44] In retrospect her statements about *The Sun Also Rises* are amusing, but they certainly were not to Ernest who felt that she had no family loyalty. Margot's response to Wilson's hunting ability is similar. First she encourages, then she undercuts. "And I want so to see you perform again. You were lovely, this morning. That is if blowing things' heads off is lovely" (SSOEH, 9). She depreciates Francis's first act of bravery—the killing of a bull buffalo—a primary step toward his achieving manhood. "'It seemed very unfair to me,' Margot said, 'chasing those big helpless things in a motor car.'" When both Wilson and Francis bathe in the warmth of their mutual experience, she intrudes to try to burst their bubble: "You're both talking rot. Just because you've chased some helpless animals in a motor car you talk like heroes" (SSOEH, 33).

Finally, as the ultimate Terrible Mother, she will not allow her son independent manhood. Once Francis has shown his courage and by extension his manhood, she extracts the ultimate sacrifice, his life.[45] Both men in the story are diminished by their association with Margot. Francis pays with his life; Wilson with whatever honor he has left. Though he has condemned Margot's character—"I've seen enough of their [American women's] damn terrorism" (SSOEH, 10)—it does not stop him from being used by her to undermine her husband's pride. After she does so, he further diminishes himself by shifting the blame to Francis, a typically childish rationalization. "What does he think I am, a bloody plaster saint? Let him keep her where she belongs. It's his own fault" (SSOEH, 23). Clearly under Margot's domination through the end of the story, he has no intention of trying to see that justice is done. Though he believes she has murdered Francis—"Why didn't you poison him? That's what they do in England"—he is ready to testify that it was an accident and have the gunbearers and driver do likewise. The extent of her capitulation is to say, "please" (SSOEH, 37).

Whether or not Margot kills Francis accidentally or on purpose is not relevant in terms of her function as a Terrible Mother.[46] What is significant is that she destroys him, either accidentally or on purpose, and she survives. The destructive power of the Terrible Mother is not always purposeful. The Earth devouring the bones of her children is not acting out of malice. Margot's strength is shown throughout the story. It is attested to by Wilson who observes, "They are . . . the hardest in the world; the cruelest, the most predatory, and the most attractive and their men have softened or gone to pieces nervously as they have hardened" (SSOEH, 8). While we need not accept Wilson's verdict, both Margot's words and her actions in the story prove him not very far from wrong. In a description of her, in an unpublished piece written 20 years after "Macomber" was published, Hemingway suggests that because Margot is very rich most of his readers would not have met her particular type of bitch.[47] The statement conjures up visions of Daisy Buchanan, another rich and destructive bitch-goddess, beautiful but deadly. And Gatsby too gets shot as a result of his relationship with her. Whether or not one accepts Wilson as a moral center for the story, there is no reason to deny his ability to judge the Macomber relationship. Speaking of Margot and other American women he says, "They govern, of course, and to govern one has to be cruel sometimes" (SSOEH, 10). In the end she governs Wilson also, and gets away with murder in the opinion of Wilson, many readers, and finally, her creator.[48] Francis has been killed, Wilson has been used, and Margot will be a very wealthy widow, very like a black widow, perhaps?

Another of Hemingway's indestructible women who is considered destructive by the man in her life is Helen of "The Snows of Kilimanjaro." Helen is a woman who has survived much. "Her husband had died when she was still a comparatively young woman." She tried devoting herself to her children; that worked for a while but then she took to drinking too much. After the drinking there was a succession of lovers, and "after she had the lovers she did not have to drink so much because she did not have to be drunk to sleep.... Then one of her two children was killed in a plane crash..." (SSOEH, 61). Helen is a courageous woman and she sets forth to rebuild her life through her relationship with Harry. She does not realize that the relationship which is good for her is destructive to him. As he is dying, Harry turns on Helen, thinking of her as the "destroyer of his talent." He tries to retaliate by undermining her assurance about their relationship, calling her a "rich bitch," telling her that "love is a dunghill." She responds with patience and kindness, replying to his barbs by telling him, "You don't have to destroy me ... I've been destroyed two or three times already. You wouldn't want to destroy me again, would you?" (SSOEH, 63). The implication here is that though Helen can seem to be destroyed, she is, in effect phoenixlike, indestructible. Having been destroyed and enduring several times before, she will survive Harry also. She has had practice. Harry, of course, does not survive, either spiritually or physically.

Helen's mothering qualities are stressed throughout the story. She is constantly busy doing for Harry. She feeds him broth (chicken soup?), tries to read to him, encourages him and tries to keep his spirits up. Parentlike, she is full of platitudes about not giving up. Like the child who blames his parents for all his ineptitudes, Harry whines about how the comfort Helen has provided has blunted the edge of his talent. When he is not rationalizing his own failure, however, he realizes that all his problems are of his own making. "Why should he blame this woman because she kept him well? He had destroyed his talent by not using it, by betrayals of himself and what he believed in, by drinking so much that he blunted the edge of his perceptions, by laziness, by sloth, and by snobbery, by pride and by prejudice, by hook and by crook" (SSOEH, 60).

As Hemingway grew older he seemed to have worked through his fear of the domination of the all-American bitch mother and the rejection of the nurse mother and developed a more positive attitude toward the possibilities of a reinforcing male/female relationship. This development follows the pattern of his personal relationships, working from his mother through Agnes to Hadley. His relationships with these women represented stepping stones in his education and as he worked through them symbolically in his fiction, he was able to put away the fears and anxieties of the testing by the Terrible Mother and move toward rapprochement with his fear of women. His relationship with Hadley illustrated to him how beneficial and reinforcing a woman could be for her man. Hadley was the prototypical nourishing mother figure in his life and his positive indestructible women are modeled after his conception of her. Unfortunately, Hemingway had to lose her in order to fully appreciate her. Perhaps it was by losing her that he was able to maintain the image of her perfection. Hemingway's male protagonists also are deprived of their nurturing women, but by death, not divorce.

At the time of his fortieth birthday Hemingway wrote Hadley that the more he saw of women, the more he admired her.[49] Significantly, it is at about this period in his life that he created his most positive indestructible women: Pilar and Maria of *For Whom the Bell Tolls*. Pilar is Hemingway's most fully drawn and interesting woman character, perhaps the only one who does not fall into one or the other of the stock patterns his heroines usually follow.[50] There is no other character in all his works quite like her. No other Hemingway woman attains the level of selfhood or individuality that Pilar does. She is the only assertive female in his works who functions in a positive manner. All of his other positive women are passive to the extreme. Why Pilar escaped this relegation to type is a matter for conjecture. The answer might lie in her role in the novel. Though she is one of the main characters, she is not the romantic heroine; Maria is. Since Pilar does not have to serve as the testing ground for Jordan's masculinity, her gender is not so threatening. She is allowed an independence and assertiveness beyond that allowed the women who provide the love interest for the hero.

Hemingway's development of Pilar's character is detailed and realistic. She defies all the critical assessments of Hemingway's women as one-dimensional.[51] What she cannot defy is critical myopia. Though she looms large in *For Whom the Bell Tolls*, a startling number of critics have managed to ignore her. Shaw's book on Hemingway devotes only two sentences to her.[52] Atkins does not mention her in a chapter devoted to the women in Hemingway's works.[53] In Whitlow's *Cassandra's Daughters* one would certainly expect some discussion of the most Cassandra-like woman in Hemingway. It is Pilar who sees Robert's death in his hand and who is the kind of "life-affirming" woman that Whitlow defines in his book. Yet he mentions her only in passing.[54] Guttman, Allen, Rovit, and Pearsall are similarly shortsighted.[55] And yet unless one chooses purposefully to disregard Pilar's significance, one cannot help but notice that she is as Waldhorn has described her, one of the "most lavishly drawn of Hemingway's women."[56] Pilar's character is rich in complexities. She is heroic, but she has fears and doubts. She commands, but she is ready to follow Jordan when necessary and even Pablo when he returns to his former self. She feels the pleasure of helping Maria and Robert expedite their relationship, while being conscious of her jealousy of what they are experiencing. She is contemplative, recounting her experiences in an attempt to understand them and herself.

On one interpretative level hers is a well-developed realistic portrait, while in terms of a mythic overstructure she also displays certain attributes of the Great Mother in her protective, nursing, and frightening aspects. Nature imagery is used to suggest Pilar's great strength and indestructible character:

Look at her walking along with those two kids. You could not get three better-looking products of Spain than those. She is like a mountain and the boy and the girl are like young trees... In spite of what has happened to the two of them they look as fresh and clean and new and untouched as though they never heard of misfortune. (FWBT, 132)

The relationship of the trees to the mountain emphasizes Pilar's role as nourishing mother; trees can grow on a mountainside. Another implication in this passage is that Pilar has been a good nurse. She has restored these young people to health in spite of the horrors that they have endured. Pilar's great strength is also suggested when Robert Jordan first sees her "brown face like a model for a granite monument" (FWBT, 33).

Robert is told how if it were not for Pilar Maria would never have been rescued and restored to health. During the retreat from the train Pilar carried Maria herself until she could no longer do so and then bullied the men into doing likewise. Pilar and Maria become mother and daughter, following in the Demeter/Persephone mythic pattern. Like Persephone, Maria has been raped. When Persephone is in the underworld, nothing will grow. Maria's hair, which is compared to a grainfield, has been shaved by the Falangists; when she is rescued by her "mother" Pilar, it begins to grow again. The oneness of mother and daughter is suggested by the fact that Pilar enjoys Maria's experiences vicariously. She questions Maria very specifically about her lovemaking, ascertaining if she has felt the magic of the earth moving, being very pleased when she finds the girl has experienced this rare phenomenon. Pilar instructs Maria in the ways of men and women together, guiding her to sexual womanhood. As Demeter controls the blossoming on earth, so Pilar controls Maria's blossoming. It is she who stage-manages Robert and Maria's relationship even to the times and places of their intimacy. She uses Robert as a balm to return Maria to health, explaining to Maria that loving someone "would take it all away" (FWBT, 63), it being the emotional scar of the rape. She uses Robert to return Maria to health, knowing he is going to die. She reads it in his hand early in their relationship. In terms of the myth, Robert is thus like the Year King or consort for the Great Goddess, who serves the goddess as husband for one year and then is sacrificed to insure the fertility of the land. Like the goddess's consort, Robert dies so the earth can be fruitful, the goddess be served.

In Pilar's relationships with the various men in her life, Hemingway illustrates the indestructibility of the female. She is a woman who has seen much and remained strong and determined. After being the mistress of three different bullfighters, she becomes the woman of Pablo. In the story of her relationship with Finito, whose name is significant in itself, the nurturing and enduring qualities of Pilar are clearly demonstrated. He is tubercular and suffers from repeated internal injuries caused by blows from the bulls' horns; Pilar stays by him, rubbing his scarred body, washing him down with alcohol, praising and encouraging him. In recalling the experience, she muses, "But neither bull force nor bull courage lasted...and what did last? I last, she thought. Yes, I have lasted"(FWBT, 183). Her history augurs well for her future. She is one who has endured and will endure.

Whereas the war and the type of guerrilla life the group is leading have temporarily "terminated" Pablo, Pilar's strength has not failed. But her endurance is not only affirmative in terms of her own fate, her strength is also important to the group. Robert Jordan realizes this: "Without the woman there is no organization nor any discipline here and with the woman it can be very good" (FWBT, 63). Pilar is what her name implies, the pillar which holds up the loosely constructed edifice of the guerrilla band. More than that she is a pillar of the Spanish people. Robert is a stranger, a foreigner who is briefly important to the cause. Pilar is of the land, a citizen, one who will remain to build the new society if there is to be one. Her endurance has greater implications for the future of the country than does his. Agustín remarks on her importance, "The Pilar is much much more than thou canst imagine" (FWBT, 277). And she is; she is on one level a brave and complex gypsy woman, but she is also a Demeter figure, the nurturing goddess, an emblem of woman's strength.[57]

Maria, on the other hand, while not as fully developed a character as Pilar, is also illustrative of woman's indestructible qualities. She is closely associated with nature; her behavior is nurturing and mothering.

The images Hemingway uses to describe her stress her connections to nature: "Her hair was the golden brown of a grain field that has been burned dark in the sun..." (FWBT, 25). Her body becomes the earth itself in Robert Jordan's perceptions as he feels "her breasts like two small hills that rise out of the long plain where there is a well, and the far country beyond the hills was the valley of her throat..." (FWBT, 321). She is like a corn goddess with the brown and the gold of the earth and of grain reflected in her eyes, "eyes [that] were the same golden tawny brown" (FWBT, 25).

Besides being described in terms that would suggest her body as one with the matter of the earth, she is also compared to the earth's natural creatures. "She walks like a colt moves" (FWBT, 133), and "She stroked under his hand like a kitten" (FWBT, 168). Throughout the book Robert calls her his "little rabbit." The connotations of fertility in that nickname are obvious. The creatures Maria is compared with are young, soft, and vulnerable and by extension, Maria would seem to be the same. She is anything but that.

Her soft exterior incases a tough inner core. The very fact that someone so physically and psychologically unprepared for the horrors that she has undergone should exhibit the strength that she does is further testimony to Hemingway's beliefs about the indestructibility of woman. Maria, who was brought up in the sheltered manner of young women in Spain, must live through the slaughter of her family. This proper young woman who was the daughter of the mayor is repeatedly raped by a regiment of Falangists. When

Joaquín tells of the slaughter of his family, he apologizes to Maria because he feels that perhaps his tale will trigger memories of her family's deaths. Her retort is "Que va . . . Mine are such a big bucket that yours falling in will never fill it" (FWBT, 135). This little rabbit is of such ferocity and determination that she carries a razor with her to cut her own throat in case she should be captured.

She shares the mothering responsibilities with Pilar, helping Pilar cook and care for the partisan band. She is solicitous of Robert, treating him so tenderly that Pilar teases her, "Must you care for him as a suckling child?" Though the situation should work to cast him in a paternal role, caring for her, the imagery here suggests that she is the mother and he is the helpless child.

There has been general disagreement among critics about Maria's role in the novel. Some have considered her as little more than a latinized Catherine Barkley, others another example of a Hemingway sexual fantasy come true.[58] The beauty of the love between Robert and Maria also acts to emphasize the ugliness of what is happening around them. The physical description of Maria could be one of Martha Gellhorn, to whom the novel is dedicated.[59] However, because of her unassertive behavior few readers have seen any other similarities between Maria and Martha. I would suggest that another similarity is in their indomitability. Hemingway had much admiration for Gellhorn's courage as they covered the Spanish Civil War together, calling her braver than most men, including himself. He taught her the different sounds of gunfire and when to fall flat.[60] Maria, too, with little training for battle, proves courageous and stalwart in the blowing of the bridge and the subsequent escape. When Robert is wounded she is ready to stay and die with him and must be forced to leave.

Maria acts also as the personification of the life principle. By participating in the mystery of sex with Maria, Robert "magically, by a simple touching of flank, of shoulders and of feet, [makes] . . . an alliance against death . . ." (FWBT, 252). In a later book Hemingway's protagonist calls the sex act "the only mystery that he believed in except the occasional bravery of man" (ARIT, 153). As much as the skeptics may deride the romanticism of the earth-moving sexual unions, it is clear that Hemingway meant for them to embody the special quality of the love affair between Maria and Robert. When they feel "the earth move out and away from under them," they become part of a select few. The uniqueness of what they experience separates them from the many and allows them to have in their brief time together what others cannot experience in a long lifetime. They have shared a transcendental moment and faced death together. Though he does not originally realize the seriousness of his feelings for her, by the time of their last day together, Robert's concern for Maria's future is expressed by his thoughts and by his deeds. When he thinks that Pablo's defection will cause the death of them all if Golz does not rescind the orders, Maria's is the escape that he is concerned about: "You are going to kill them all off with those orders. Maria too. You'll kill her too with those orders. Can't you even get her out of it?" After the bridge is blown, he tries to make her cross the road second so she will be in the safest position.

Maria's significance as a positive female principle is expressed by Robert and by the narrator. The description of their caresses is that he holds her "tight as though she were all of life" and she is all of female life to him: "Maria is my true love and my wife. I never had a true love. I never had a wife. She is also my sister and I never had a sister, and my daughter, and I never will have a daughter" (FWBT, 333). Maria is one woman; Maria is all women; she is the life force.

If there is any way to read the ending of *For Whom the Bell Tolls* optimistically, it must take into account the roles that Pilar and Maria play in the novel. Robert Jordan is an American who has come to fight in the Spanish Civil War because he loves the country and its people. If he is fighting for anything it is for their right of self-determination. Maria and Pilar are Spain. In an earlier passage Robert expresses the thought that one could not find better-looking products of the country than Pilar, Maria, and Joaquín. As Joaquín is dead, Maria and Pilar are the remaining representatives of the country's best.

Though Hemingway shows us clearly that the blowing of the bridge is probably useless to the cause and many lives have been lost needlessly in the process, the fact that Maria, Pilar, Pablo, Agustín, Rafael, and Primitivo survive provides what little hope there is. Robert Jordan is not a religious man and he does not believe in an afterlife. However, when he is wounded, his rationale for making Maria leave him is that as they are one, if she goes then he will be going with her: "As long as there is one of us, there is both of us. Thou art me too now. Thou art all there will be of me" (FWBT, 435–36). When she leaves, he wants to believe it is true. "Try to believe what you told her. That is the best. And who says it is not true? Not you."

Regardless of whether or not one accepts the notion that Robert's immortality will be in his oneness with Maria, one is sure as Robert is sure that "Pilar will take care of her [Maria] as well as any one can." As Robert is sure that Maria will be fine because Pilar will take care of her, so the reader can predict that Maria, the daughter, will become as Pilar, the mother, strong, courageous, and indestructible. Pilar and Maria will endure.

Renata, the docile daughter-mistress of *Across the River and into the Trees,* is the final beneficial and indestructible female in Hemingway's works. Like his other passive females, she has been criticized for the shallowness of her conception. Maxwell Geismar says, "She is a fantasy of the completely docile, pliant child bride and is useful in the novel merely as interlocutor for the Colonel's overwhelming narcissism."[61] Norman Cousins deplores her characterization as one "unrecognizable as a person and who exists solely for the reminiscent intellectual and sensual pleasures of the hero-soldier."[62] Adriana Ivancich, the woman who is generally acknowledged to be the model for Renata, evaluated the character of Renata as boring, commenting that "A girl like that does not exist."[63] Whether or not Renata is a realistically depicted character is beside the point when evaluating her in terms of Hemingway's tendency to create female characters of enduring and indestructible natures.

Like Maria before her, Renata functions as the symbol of some kind of immortality for a man who is about to die. Even her name suggests rebirth. Colonel Cantwell calls her daughter, though she is not his biological daughter. Considering their relative ages, she could well be his granddaughter. The big difference in their ages contributes to the reader's sense that Renata holds the key to the future. She is two generations removed from the colonel and as such is spiritually closer to him than she would be to the middle generation; popular wisdom has it that the generation gap is not as great between grandparents and grandchildren as it is between parents and children. So as one generation passes its values to the next, as grandchildren learn history at the knee of their grandparents, so Cantwell spends most of the novel recounting his history to Renata. She accepts his opinions about everything from lobsters to the soldiering abilities of the various Allied generals in World War II. She is his spiritual inheritor because she becomes the living repository of all his thoughts and feelings. In this way some of him will live on through her. At the end of the novel, when he dies, Cantwell like Jordan knows that Renata will survive. He even sends his love through an emissary who will, perhaps, supplant him.

Renata, like others of Hemingway's indestructible women, is lover, daughter, and mother in one. In her role as protecting and nurturing mother, she makes sure that Cantwell takes his medicine on time. She is constantly correcting his behavior and his bawdy language. "Please don't be rough" is her byword (ARIT, 114). When she gives him a gift, she instructs him as to the proper response: "Now say thank you" (ARIT, 104).

Mythically, her character is aligned with both Aphrodite and the moon goddess. Aphrodite was created out of the foam that formed around the genitals of Uranus that had been thrown into the sea by Cronos. Just as in the myth Cronos (Time) castrated Uranus, so in the novel time is the enemy who will cut down Cantwell. Uranus's deposal, however, is the cause of the birth of Aphrodite. Hemingway underlines the mythic allusion by having Renata give Cantwell a portrait of herself in which she is depicted as Aphrodite rising from the waves. In another scene in the novel, Renata identifies herself with the moon goddess. Correcting Cantwell who tells her, "And you're the sun," she says "I want to be the moon, too." Her identification with the moon is based on her sense of the moon being female and a female who has suffered and undergone much. She says, "I'll be the moon. She has many troubles too"

(ARIT, 99). The moon, however, as Cantwell explains, has been around a long time and if she wanes, she also waxes before she wanes.

If the character of Renata is isolated from her various mythological and symbolic functions in the novel and merely analyzed as the portrait of a 19-year-old young woman, then her remarkable strength is more apparent. She is little more than a girl, still in her teens, in love with a man who is over 50 and moribund, hardly an optimistic prospect. The suggestion is implicit in the novel that this 19-year-old has the maturity and durability to handle this difficult situation and survive unscarred. While she exhibits every capability of accomplishing this on her own, Cantwell helps in the process by symbolically cutting all ties that would link them. He sees to it that the mementos she has given him will be returned after his death. These mementos, which include the portrait of Renata as Aphrodite, are to go to her along with his love, which Alvarito is to deliver.

Renata exhibits great self-possession and maturity in her dealings with Cantwell. She has few illusions about the future of their affair. When Cantwell says, "Then let us be married at once," she replies, "No, I had to make a decision about that, as about the other different things" (ARIT, 118). While they joke about living together, Renata suggests that the reason she will not marry Cantwell is that she does not want to be married many times like the movie people in Rome. When Cantwell doesn't take her allusion well, she soothes him with, "But I will love you, whatever that means, and you and I know what it means very well, as long as either of us is alive and after" (ARIT, 128). Cantwell tells her that he feels armored by her love.

By assuring Cantwell of her love, Renata acts as a balm and palliative for his last days. The colonel doubts that one can love very much after death, but Renata reassures him that she will endeavor to do so. "I don't know whether you can either. But I will try. Don't you feel better to be loved?" The colonel is not a man with many illusions about life's difficulties, but he does rate Renata's love as a positive value. He includes her as one of his ilk, telling her that "all people such as us" have the desire to command. She acknowledges the compliment and says, "Thank you for the such as us."

Cantwell dies at the end of the novel, having said good-bye to Renata. If there is hope for the future, it is personified in Renata, who, young and durable, is one of the few optimistic notes in this otherwise depressing deathwatch.

Though Renata is generally conceded to be Hemingway's final positive heroine, Earl Rovit suggests still another. Rovit sees Hemingway's heroines as purified mother figures. However, he sees a regression in their depiction. In Rovit's interpretation Hemingway's heroine has regressed so completely by his last novel that the "heroine (the mother and anima) has assumed its primordial symbolic shape as la mer, the eternal feminine sea."[64] Rovit's reading has merit. There *is* a regression in Hemingway's characterization of women. That regression is from the more complex, modern women, such as Lady Brett Ashley who is one of the "chaps" or Margot Macomber who must "govern" to the more primitive sorts like Maria and Renata who in their relationships with men articulate their desire for union and to serve. Besides being explained biographically, this regression can also be read as an expression of Hemingway's philosophical "primitivism."

There is general agreement that "primitive" is a relevant description of Hemingway, but there is general disagreement about what is meant by that appellation. Young states that "Hemingway's book is the mainline of development of one of our minor literary traditions, in which naturalism goes primitive."[65] Burnam suggests a connection between primitivism and the masculine ethic so prevalent in Hemingway. "Hemingway's men are men and they involve themselves constantly with such obviously elemental things as death and sex; their approach is masculine, direct, even brutal; they cut through the complexities of contemporary society to the so-called 'primal' drives."[66] In a study that compares Faulkner and Hemingway, Sister Mary Damascene Brocki delineates comparable anticivilizational, hence "primitive" attitudes in both of them. Both advocate new possibilities for moral freedom in the wilderness or wide sea, "both unspoiled areas where men may exercise a genuine and radical freedom in exploring and in discovering what is good and what is true."[67] By extension, this anticivilizational attitude accounts for the indestructible qualities of women, who in Hemingway's depiction are the least civilized, the least affected by intellectual agonies.

Hemingway's indestructible women are often described with imagery which allies them to the earth and its animal creatures, both tame and savage. Nature is a positive value for Hemingway. Though it can be threatening, it is an obvious testing ground for man's courage and tenacity. Just as Hemingway uses the forest, the jungle or the sea as a backdrop against which to test the individual, so woman functions in an analogous manner. *The Sun Also Rises* provides a clue about Hemingway's attitude. The novel was perceived as a depiction of Hemingway's generation because of the quotation from Gertrude Stein which precedes the story: "You are all a lost generation." Hemingway, however, tried to balance the pessimistic implication of that statement by following it with a quotation from Ecclesiastes: "One generation passeth away, and another generation cometh; but the earth abideth forever." Hemingway's works are full of "lost" individuals, but even among the lost he saw hope for the future. In *A Moveable Feast* Hemingway tells us that the pessimism implicit in Miss Stein's quotation troubled him until he returned to his home. When he saw his wife Hadley, his son Bumby, and his cat, his sense of despair was dispelled. The woman, the child, and the small creature of nature caused him to put faith in the natural cycle—in the endurance of life through the generations that follow each other, in the fact that the earth abideth.

4

Steinbeck

The three authors discussed in this book may be similar in some ways, but obviously there are more differences than similarities in their works. Because of these differences they project their conceptions about the indestructible woman in widely varying ways. There are no female characters in Steinbeck who match the lush sensuality of the goddesslike Eula Varner or who are wounded fighting in foreign wars as Linda Snopes was; nor is there a Steinbeck heroine with the worldly sophistication and pizzazz to match Brett Ashley's or the unusual maturity of the 19-year-old Renata. Faulkner's women are limited regionally; they are all Southerners. The majority of Hemingway's significant heroines are continentals or Americans living or working abroad. Steinbeck's female characters come from a variety of geographical locations in the United States and Mexico. While geography is not necessarily a sound basis for literary differentiation, in the case of these three authors it is important because setting plays such an important part in their themes. More significantly, since all are primitivists, albeit of differing orthodoxy, the land functions as a positive value in all of their works. Where the various indestructible women are described in terms of nature imagery, or where they function as earth goddess types, there is a correlation in the ways that Faulkner, Hemingway, and Steinbeck portray them. That is perhaps the only similarity in the way these three men depict the indestructible woman.

John Ditsky suggests that there are certain parallels in Faulkner's and Steinbeck's treatment of nature in relation to character, but that there are more outstanding differences, the basic difference being that Faulkner is consistent in his use of attitude toward the land as a criterion for judging human worth, while Steinbeck is not.[1] Faulkner's "basically agrarian principles" dominate his thinking from his earliest works through his Nobel Prize address. "Furthermore," explains Ditsky, "there is a strong possibility that serious differences emerged from Steinbeck's evident desire never to write the same type of book twice, while Faulkner saw himself as trying repeatedly to get one book written successfully."[2] Perhaps the fact that Faulkner lived on the land and saw himself as a farmer contributed to his consistent concern with and attitude toward the land. Though Steinbeck did some farm work as a boy and young man, his movement when he started writing was in an urban direction; he launched his married life in Pacific Grove and later lived in New York City. Since Faulkner's works embody a criterion that judges people by their coherence with natural processes, women, as closely attuned to these processes, are seen as enduring. Some of Steinbeck's women fall into a similar classification.

Faulkner works in one setting inhabited by a variety of character types; Hemingway uses one predominant plot pattern and protagonist type. When discussing Steinbeck's works, however, most critics stress the diversity of both technique and subject matter. Nevertheless there are certain consistencies in his works. Lester Jay Marks in his thoughtful evaluation of thematic design in Steinbeck's novels suggests three recurring thematic patterns. One of these patterns proposes that humankind may be viewed biologically, as a "group animal" composed of individuals ("cells") but having a will and intelligence of its own, distinct from any one of its parts.[3] Most of the enduring women in Steinbeck derive their positive value from the fact that they act as the nurturing and reproductive machinery of the group. Their optimistic significance lies, not in their individual spiritual triumph, but in their function as perpetuators of the species. They are not judged by any biblical or traditional sense of morality. The Hemingway credo may maintain that immorality was what made you feel disgusted afterward; the Steinbeck credo reads that perhaps there is no such thing as sin, only how people are. Those people who act for the good of the group or the greatest number, in whatever manner, are those whose behavior is valued. A number of Steinbeck's indestructible women function within that ethical construct.

During the writing of this book, I was asked by students and colleagues about the subject of my research. The reply that I was analyzing a character type which I had chosen to call the indestructible woman in the works of Faulkner, Hemingway, and Steinbeck brought forth a standard response. "Well, there is Ma Joad, but who else?" Ma Joad is perhaps the most easily recognizable example of the type. Her characterization is so unabashedly representative of these writers' attitude toward the indestructibility of woman that were it not for the fact that she follows rather than precedes others of her type in their works, she might be called the archetype of the breed in American fiction.

In terms of overwhelming odds, both physical and mental, none of the other characters covered in this study has quite as much to endure as Ma Joad. The novel begins with her being uprooted from her home, having her center of being capsized. When her son Tom comments on the resultant change in her character, she explains, "I never had my house pushed over . . . I never had my fambly stuck out on the road. I never had to sell—ever'thing—" (GW, 66). Not only is her home destroyed, but she must, because of the limited space in the truck, burn her mementos, her relics of the past. This she does of her own accord, privately, and without letting the others see the pain it causes her.

After losing her home and the tokens of the past, Ma must endure a series of deaths and hardships. First Grandpa does not survive the uprooting. Ma's compassion is displayed during Grandma's illness as Ma strives to make her comfortable, fanning Grandma, tending to her. Then Grandma succumbs. Ma's behavior on the occasion of Grandma's death is illustrative of her great compassion and personal indomitability. Ma also acts to impart to Rose of Sharon the need for responsibility and sharing, encouraging her daughter to fan Grandma also during her final illness. Because Ma is aware of the family need for her as a citadel of strength, she cannot even openly display her anguish. "Rose of Sharon watched her secretly. And when she saw Ma fighting with her face, Rose of Sharon closed her eyes and pretended to be asleep" (GW, 190). Ma is so thoroughly dedicated to the good of the greater number that she lies all night with Grandma's dead body in her arms until the group gets across the state border and the California desert. The toll of this deed shows: "Her face was stiff and putty-like, and her eyes seemed to have sunk deep into her head, and the rims were red with weariness" (GW, 203). Even after the family has made it across and Ma tells them why she did what she did, she does not break down. As Tom moves to comfort her, she says, "Don't touch me.... I'll hol' up if you don't touch me. That'd get me" (GW, 204).

All those in contact with her are aware of Ma's awesome indestructibility. "The family looked at Ma with a little terror at her strength" (GW, 203). Casey assesses the enormity of Ma's deed: "All night long, an' she was alone. Johnny there's a woman so great with love—she scares me. Makes me afraid an' mean" (GW, 204).

Grandma's death is only the beginning of the trial Ma has to face. More deaths and departures follow. Noah decides to desert the group. The Wilsons must be left behind; Connie leaves. Casey is killed and Tom becomes a fugitive. Rose of Sharon's baby is born dead. All around them there is starvation and deprivation, harassment and hostility. To add to these disasters a flood forces what's left of the family to abandon their camp. Through all this Ma remains strong and steadfast.

Ma Joad stands out in Steinbeck's works as a complete and positive characterization of a woman. Few of his other women are so fully drawn. None of his other women functions on so many interpretive levels, all affirmative. Not only is Ma realistically characterized as a believable woman, but she is also the embodiment of the myth of the pioneer woman, the symbol for positive motherhood, and the earth goddess incarnate. In a writer whose works are criticized for their preponderance of misfits, aberrations, and cripples, the characterization of Ma Joad's strength and goodness is a positive statement about the quality possible in the female.

Throughout the novel, Ma Joad functions as a nurturing mother to all. The fact that she is known only as "Ma" and is not given a first name reinforces her maternal image. The reader is first introduced to her while she is preparing food for the family, the traditional job of the mother. Not only does she prepare food for her own family, but she also welcomes strangers and offers to share with them whatever she has. She has baked bread, the staff of life, and symbolically she is the provider of both life and its sustenance. The image is of Mother Earth or Lady Bountiful. Her description emphasizes her maternal role. "Ma was heavy, but not fat; thick with child-bearing and work. She wore a loose Mother Hubbard of gray cloth in which there had once been colored flowers..." (GW, 64).

Ma mothers not only her biological children, but any and all who are in need of care. She even mothers Grandma and Grandpa, chasing Grandpa down to button his pants as if he were a little boy, seeing to Grandma's needs. Her Mother Earth image is strongly reinforced by the scene where she feeds the starving children who gather around her kettle. Though there is not enough to feed her family adequately, she ladles small portions so as to leave some for the children. In every situation in the novel, Ma is ready to share whatever she has with those in need; her way of being is mothering.

In the scenes of Ma chasing down Grandpa or suffering because she does not have enough to provide for both her family and the hungry children in the camp, Ma is dramatically depicted in a realistic way. However, Steinbeck, who explained in a letter to his editor Pascal Covici that the novel had five layers, acquaints readers with Ma's archetypal role very early in the story. His initial description of her stresses her superhuman qualities. She is called "the citadel of the family, the strong place that could not be taken" (GW, 64). Her position as wise and healing goddess also makes her the family judge. Her reaction to all this distances her from the ordinary mortals in the family. She becomes an ideal; everyone looks to her for guidance. Her affirmative and indestructible qualities are accentuated:

> Her hazel eyes seemed to have experienced all possible tragedy and to have mounted pain and suffering like steps into a high calm and a superhuman understanding. She seemed to know, to accept, to welcome her position.... And since old Tom and the children could not know hurt or fear unless she acknowledged hurt and fear, she had practised denying them in herself. And since, when a joyful thing happened, they looked to see whether joy was on her, it was her habit to build up laughter out of inadequate materials. But better than joy was the calm. Imperturbability could be depended upon. And from her great and humble position in the family she had taken dignity and a clean calm beauty. From her position as healer, her hands had grown sure and cool and quiet; from her position as arbiter she had become as remote and faultless in judgment as a goddess. (GW, 64)

Ma knows that she is the foundation of the family; they stand or fall on the basis of her strength. Steinbeck makes that clear.

But Ma's characterization transcends the mythic, as mythic characters tend to be flat and static. Her characterization, both narrative and dramatic, is multidimensional. Her character rises from the pages of the book as much more than Mother Earth or serene and aloof goddess. She is both leader and follower, a wise yet ignorant woman, simple in many ways and still complex. Hers is a fully developed realistic portrait, notwithstanding those critics who think she is too good to be true.[4] Her strengths as a person are enhanced because Steinbeck chooses to show us, along with those situations in which she behaves heroically, examples of her weaknesses and doubts.

Although she behaves bravely, Ma also expresses her fears. Her bravery is not of the foolhardy kind where actions arise instinctually without forethought. Ma has the intelligence to be frightened, but to act in spite of her fears. When Al asks her if she is afraid, she responds, "A little . . . Only it ain't like scaired so much. I'm jus' a settin' here waitin'. When somepin happens that I got to do somepin—I'll do it" (GW, 108). She also expresses her fear to Tom; in this case it is the fear that his departure will undermine the already weakened family structure. "We're crackin' up, Tom. There ain't no fambly now" (GW, 310).

Like any human being she fantasizes about the future, making plans for money that is yet unearned. "I wonder—that is if we all get jobs an' all work—maybe we can get one of them little white houses" (GW, 79). In the government camp, uplifted by the sanitary conditions and hospitable reception, Ma dreams of a stove, a tent, and secondhand springs for the bed (GW, 285). Her sights are set progressively lower as fewer and fewer of her initial expectations are met. In the latter part of the novel she expresses her desire for even temporary housing: "'F we pick plenty peaches we might get a house, pay rent even, for a couple months" (GW, 326).

Steinbeck's fully rounded portrait of this indestructible woman includes instances of her ignorance, suspicion, and pride. Having never seen bathroom facilities such as those at the government camp, she inadvertently ends up in the men's room. Her country background and pride make her suspicious of strangers and wary. She rejects the camp manager's friendly overtures until she is sure of his purpose. She is not free of a little family pride, boasting of the Joad lineage, "We're Joads. We don't look up to nobody. Grampa's grampa, he fit in the Revolution. We was farm people till the debt" (GW, 274). She is nostalgic about the past, reminiscing with Rose of Sharon about her younger days. "Maybe you wouldn' think it, but your Pa was as nice a dancer as I ever seen, when he was young" (GW, 304).

While Hemingway often equates female passivity with the positive indestructible qualities of women, Steinbeck creates a number of indestructible women who are active and assertive. Ma Joad is both. She displays a number of traditionally masculine qualities without losing her womanly image. Pa Joad recounts with pride the story of how Ma "beat the hell out of a tin peddler with a live chicken." The story is humorous, but it serves as a foreshadowing for Ma Joad's future situation.

> An' Ma ain't nobody you can push aroun' neither. I seen her beat hell out of a tin peddler with a live chicken once 'cause he give her an argument. She had the chicken in one han', an' the ax in the other, about to cut its head off. She aimed to go for that peddler with the ax, but she forgot which hand was which, an' she takes after him with the chicken. Couldn' even eat that chicken when she got done. They wasn't nothing but a pair a legs in her han'. (GW, 40)

Though Ma struggles against those forces which are destroying her family, her weapons prove to be as ineffective as a live chicken. She fights with all her might and is left with little more than an inedible pair of chicken legs.

Another scene that emphasizes Ma's forceful qualities is when she challenges Pa with a jack handle. Whereas in Hemingway's stories the female who threatens male authority is a destructive force, in a number of Steinbeck's works women assume the authoritative role for the good of the group. Ma not only challenges patriarchal authority but she does it in a traditionally masculine way, by a challenge to one-to-one combat. When Pa and Tom have decided that the group should split up, Casey and Tom remaining with the Wilsons, Ma balks. "I ain't a-gonna go," she says as she balances the jack handle in her hand.

> And now Ma's mouth set hard. She said softly, "on'y way you gonna get me to go is whup me." She moved the jack handle gently again. "An' I'll shame you Pa. I won't take no whuppin', cryin' an' a-beggin'. I'll light into you. An' you ain't so sure you can whup me anyways. An' if ya do get me, I swear to God I'll wait till you got your back turned, or you're gettin' down, an' I'll knock you belly-up with a bucket, I swear to Holy Jesus' sake I will. (GW, 149)

Ma's challenge is made to prevent the weakening of the group structure, not for personal power. The fact that she acts on instinct as an agent for group preservation is underlined by her surprise at what she has done. Once the group realizes that she has taken control, that she is the power, they decide not to try to fight her. Tom reasons that even if he and Pa and the whole group try to rush Ma, it wouldn't do any good and so he says, "You win, Ma. Put away that jack handle 'fore you hurt somebody." At this point, Ma, who has been acting instinctually, comes out of her trance. "Ma looked in astonishment at the bar of iron. Her hand trembled. She dropped her weapon on the ground..." (GW, 158).

Ma Joad is not the only indestructible woman in *The Grapes of Wrath*.

Just as Faulkner used the Demeter/Persephone myth to suggest a pattern of continuity and resurrection in the relationship of mother and daughter, so in his development of Ma Joad and her daugher Rose of Sharon Steinbeck too plays on the theme of the endless renewal of the female principle. Though Levant claims that the final scene of the novel is a disaster because, among other things, "there is no preparation for Rose of Sharon's transformation," all through the story Steinbeck shows us Ma instructing Rose of Sharon and teaching her through precept and example nourishing and reinforcing behavior patterns.[5] Rose of Sharon, who prior to the beginning of the story had been "a plump, passionate hoyden," is changed by her pregnancy. As the child grows within her, and she prepares to convert her role from daughter to mother, she becomes "balanced, careful, wise." Her whole thought and action turn inward and she in consumed with her sense of self as potential mother, as a reproductive agent (GW, 83). At the beginning of the trip to California Connie and Rose of Sharon share a universe of their own: "The world had drawn close around them, and they were the center of it, or rather Rose of Sharon was in the center of it with Connie making a small orbit around her" (GW, 113). Harshly, they are blasted out of their selfish cycles. Connie behaves badly, abandoning both the family and group effort as well as his wife and expected child. Rose of Sharon, on the other hand, endures many deprivations and deaths and by the end of the novel is ready to take her place beside Ma as a pillar of the family.

Rose of Sharon prepares for this role in a number of ways. She aids Ma with the care of the dying Grandma. She helps not only with care of the dying but also with nourishing the living. Even when she is feeling very weak as a result of both malnutrition and pregnancy, she tries to help with the cooking and cleaning chores. "I oughta help Ma... I tried, but ever' time I stirred about I throwed up" (GW, 224). Bedraggled and burdened, deserted by her husband, Rose of Sharon still drags herself out of bed to do her part in earning money for the support of the family. Sick and weak, she insists on participating in the cotton picking. Ma tries to dissuade her, but she is adamant.

> The girl set her jaw. "I'm a-goin', she said.
> "Ma, I got to go."
> "Well, you got no cotton sack. You can't pull no sack."
> "I'll pick into your sack."
> "I wisht you wouldn'."
> "I'm a-goin'." (GW, 383)

Rose of Sharon goes to pick cotton with the family in her weakened state and becomes even more worn out. Her eyes lose their luster. She shivers and her knees buckle, but she holds her head high (GW, 384).

Ma instructs Rose of Sharon about her responsibilities in the cycle of life. She explains the terror, the loneliness, and the joy of woman's lot. In Ma's philosophy the hurt and the pain do not matter because they are part of the continuity of the species. The eternal cycle of womanhood is represented in a scene where Grandma, Ma, and Rose of Sharon are together in a tent: Grandma is dying; Ma is caring for her; Rose of Sharon is pregnant. Ma uses the occasion to prepare Rose of Sharon for what being a woman entails:

> Ma raised her eyes to the girl's face. Ma's eyes were patient, but the lines of strain were on her forehead... "When you're young, Rosasharn, ever'thing that happens is a thing all by itself. It's a lonely thing. I know, I 'member, Rosasharn." Her mouth loved the name of her daughter. "You gonna have a baby, Rosasharn, and that's somepin to you lonely and away. That's gonna hurt you, an' the hurt'll be lonely hurt, an' this tent is alone in the worl', Rosasharn."(GW, 186)

But while Ma acknowledges the pain and the loneliness that are in store for Rose of Sharon, she also tries to share with her daughter her ability to transcend those experiences.

> And Ma went on, "They's a time of change, an' when that comes, dyin' is a piece of all dyin', and bearin' is a piece of all bearin', an' bearin' an' dyin' is two pieces of the same thing. An' then things ain't lonely any more, Rosasharn. I wisht I would tell you so you'd know, but I can't." And her voice was so soft, so full of love, that tears crowded into Rose of Sharon's eyes, and flowed over her eyes and blinded her. (GW, 186)

Rose of Sharon's tears show that she has been touched by Ma's explanation.

Steinbeck shows us Ma infusing Rose of Sharon with her own strength and indomitability. In two particularly meaningful scenes, Ma symbolically passes the torch to Rose of Sharon. In the first of these scenes, the torch is passed by means of an icon, earrings, an appropriately feminine symbol. In this scene Rose of Sharon is initially shown in a deep depression, moving sluggishly about her work. She has been nibbling on a piece of slack lime because of the lack of calcium in her diet. She is sick, lonely, deserted, and fears the effect of this situation on her unborn child: "Rose of Sharon said dully, 'If Connie hadn' went away, we'd a had a little house by now, with him studyin' an' all. Would a got milk like I need. Would a had a nice baby. This here baby ain't gonna be no good. I ought a had milk.'" (GW, 315). To force her out of her lethargy and coax her out of her pessimistic stance, Ma gives her a pair of small gold earrings that are one of the few things she has painfully salvaged from the past. In order to wear the earrings, however, Rose of Sharon must bear the pain of having her ears pierced. Symbolically, she must suffer to prove herself ready to assume Ma's responsibilities and position. Lest we miss the import of this scene, Steinbeck underlines it for us. Rose of Sharon asks, "Does it mean somepin?" Ma answers, "Why, 'course it does... 'Course it does" (GW, 316).

The final scene in the book is the other significant indicator that Rose of Sharon will succeed Ma as enduring matriarch, indestructible woman. The scene has been problematic for critics. Steinbeck's editor, Pascal Covici, tried in his diplomatic manner to get Steinbeck to rethink it. "No one could fail to be moved by the incident of Rose of Sharon giving her breast to the dying man," wrote Covici, "yet, taken as the finale of such a book with all its vastness and surge, it struck us on reflection as being too abrupt."[6] But Steinbeck would not be swayed. He wanted the scene as it was for a number of reasons: first, he saw the action as "a survival symbol not a love symbol"; second, he did not want the reader to come away from the story satisfied, for he had done his damndest "to rip a reader's nerves to rags." As for the genesis of the action, Steinbeck explained, "The incident of the earth mother feeding by the breast is older than literature."[7]

Response to this scene had been varied. Steinbeck was amazed at how few critics understood it.[8] Martin Shockley sees the scene in terms of Christian theology, suggesting that Rose of Sharon becomes a Christ figure:

> The meaning of this incident, Steinbeck's final paragraph, is clear in terms of Christian symbolism . . . Rosasharn gives what Christ gave, what we receive in memory of Him. The ultimate mystery of the Christian religion is realized as Rosasharn "Looked up and across the barn, and her lips came together and smiled mysteriously." *This is My body,* says Rosasharn, and becomes the Resurrection and the Life. Rose of Sharon, the life-giver, symbolizes the resurrective aspect of Christ. . . . In her, death and life are one, and through her, life triumphs over death.[9]

Eric W. Carlson disagrees with any analysis which attempts to cram a stark, primal symbol into the mold of orthodox Christian symbolism and doctrine. He can accept an interpretation which sees Rose of Sharon's act as symbolically transmuting her maternal love into a love of all people. He sees the final scene as "symbolizing the main theme of the novel: the prime function of life is to nourish life."[10] Numerous others have presented their viewpoints on both the significance and the efficacy of this final scene.[11] Howard Levant calls it "the nadir of bad Steinbeck," because of his claim that Steinbeck did not foreshadow the scene, having given the reader no preparation for his "forcing Rose of Sharon into an unprepared and purely formalistic role."[12] My previous argument should illustrate that Steinbeck did prepare the reader for Rose of Sharon's assumption of Ma's mantle. But whether the critic thinks that the scene is one of tawdry fake symbolism, symbolic of the Eucharist, representative of the rapprochement with the transcendental oversoul, or in keeping with ancient analogies of the behavior of virtuous women, they are all in agreement that the scene has optimistic and positive implications.

Two things in the scene argue strongly for an interpretation that includes Rose of Sharon among Steinbeck's indestructible women. First, Rose of Sharon has become an extension of Ma. As in the Demeter/Persephone myth, the daughter has become the mother. Having experienced great pain, she has been forged as Ma has, through suffering. A parity between the two women has been established. Up until this point in the novel, Rose of Sharon is always referred to as a girl, but in the narrative description of this final scene, Steinbeck emphasizes the equal status of the pair: "and the two women looked deep into each other." In the bulk of the novel, Ma has been the nourisher, the one who sees to the feeding of family and strangers. In this scene, though Ma is the instigator, she cannot do the feeding. It must be Rose of Sharon. By giving her breast to the old man, Rose of Sharon takes her place with Ma as earth goddess. Her youth and fertility combine with her selfless act to signify continuity and hope.

The second idea that should be stressed here is the sex of Steinbeck's symbols of hope and fortitude, Ma Joad and Rose of Sharon. Throughout the novel Steinbeck emphasizes the special indestructibility of women. When the men are disheartened and defeated, the women bear up and take charge. Pa comments on this phenomenon twice. As the family is mired in the comfort of the Weedpatch camp, it is Ma who demands affirmative action. The relative comfort of the camp does not lull her into complacency. She knows that they cannot continue without adequate food or work. "We got to do somepin.... You're scairt to talk. An' the money is gone. You're scairt to talk it out. Ever' night you jes' eat, then you get wanderin' away.... Now don't none of you get up till we figger somepin out" (GW, 311–12). When the men voice their discouragement, Ma remonstrates, "You ain't got the right to get discouraged. This here fambly's goin' under. You jus' ain't got the right" (GW, 312). It is not because she does not feel the same things the men feel, though many critics who cannot accept her strength as realistic ignore the scenes when Ma's vulnerability shows. She never lets her weakness show because she knows the effect that would have on the family. When, after her ordeal with Grandma, Jim Casy says, "She looks tar'd ... Real tar'd like she's sick— tar'd," she hears his words and immediately reacts. "Slowly her relaxed face tightened, and the lines disappeared from the taut muscular face. Her eyes sharpened and her shoulders straightened" (GW, 95).

In the scene where Ma forces the family out of their lethargy, Pa comments, "Time was when a man said what we'd do. Seems like women is tellin' now. Seems like it's purty near time to get out a stick" (GW, 313). Ma's reaction to this speech illustrates her special kind of authority, an authority which meets the demands of the time:

> Times when they's food an' a place to set, then maybe you can use your stick an' keep your skin whole. But you ain't a-doin' your job, either a-thinkin' or a-workin'. If you was, why, you could use your stick, an' women folks'd sniffle their nose an' creep-mouse aroun'. But you just get out a stick now an' you ain't lickin' no woman you're a-fightin', cause I got a stick all laid out too. (GW, 313)

In her response to Pa she speaks not only for herself but for all women. The implication of her statement is that women will be subservient in the good times when there is plenty and the men are providing, but that in times of deprivation, a woman's true character, a commanding one, will out. In hard times, women are not only just as tough, but probably tougher than men.

In one of the final scenes of the book, after Ma has had to send Tom away, Mr. Wainwright comes to the family because he is concerned about the possibility that his daughter Aggie may become pregnant. Aggie and Al have been walking out every night and Mr. Wainwright does not want any shame to come to his family. Ma speaks up, assuring Mr. Wainwright that Pa will talk to Al, "Or if Pa won't, I will." Realizing that she has usurped Pa's place, Ma apologizes, but Pa assures her that he realizes that she meant no harm. He is disheartened: "I ain't no good anymore... Funny! Women takin' over the fambly. Woman sayin' we'll do this here, an we'll go there. An I don' even care" (GW, 377–78).

Just as Pablo in *For Whom the Bell Tolls* is "terminated," at least temporarily, by the life of the guerrilla band and Pilar takes over as commander of the group, so Pa too is undone by the uprooting of his family and Ma must take over. Leonard Lutwack has noted that Ma Joad, Pilar, and Dilsey all function in similar ways in the novels that they inhabit. In his exploration of the epic tradition in twentieth-century American fiction, he focuses on their roles as mother goddesses inspiring and protecting their hero sons.[13] There are many other similarities between Ma Joad and Pilar.[14] They are certainly two of the most fully drawn of the indestructible women created by these two authors. Why do these women survive when others succumb? Why are they able to command in times of crisis and then turn over the reins of authority to their men when the men can once again cope?

Hemingway does not provide any clues, nor do his characters see the situation as having anything to do with gender. Steinbeck, on the other hand, in both his narration and through his characters proffers generalizations about the differences in the sexes' abilities to cope with change and disaster. Ma, whose wisdom on most matters is respected by both her creator and her family, explains the reason that the women are more enduring than the men. "Woman can change better'n a man," she says (GW, 378). When Pa is ready to give up and sees no hope for the future, Ma articulates her conception of an essential difference between the way men and women handle rites of passage:

Man, he lives in jerks—baby born an' a man dies, an that's a jerk—gets a farm an' loses his farm, an' that's a jerk. Woman, it's all one flow, like a stream, little eddies, little waterfalls, but the river, it goes right on. Woman looks at it like that. We ain't gonna die out. People is goin' on—changin' a little, maybe, but goin' right on." (GW, 378)

The analogy between woman and a river is an apt one for this self-characterization by an indestructible woman. Like the river, like the stream of life, she goes on. She is allied to the natural flow of things.

Steinbeck's controversial ending is in keeping with a theme he sounds throughout this novel and in others of his works. In *The Grapes of Wrath* Steinbeck chooses two women to act as his symbols for survival. The objects of their ministrations are two men. Ma Joad and Rose of Sharon in the midst of rain and flood behave in the manner described by Ma as woman's way—like a river, they go right on.

Ma Joad's significance has been universally acclaimed. Even in the film version of Steinbeck's novel where her role is greatly reduced and the breastfeeding scene is excluded, Ma's speech about the people going on still sounds an optimistic note for the future of not only the family, but all people. As a character, Ma has received a good deal of critical attention. The same cannot be said about Juana in *The Pearl*.

As a representative of Steinbeck's theme of women's strength and endurance, Juana may be second only to Ma Joad. A possible reason for the dearth of attention to Juana's character may be that the fablelike quality of the novel does not invite analysis of character development, little of that being necessary in parables. However, parables do reduce things to essentials and the characters in them do represent large groups of people. Therefore, it is strange that in this story, which has only three characters, a man, a woman, and a baby, the woman has received such cursory critical notice. Marks mentions her only in passing, noting that the pearl causes Kino "a spiritual estrangement from his wife."[15] This oversight is all the more glaring since he is careful to quote Steinbeck's dictum that in such parables "there are only good and bad things and black and white things" (P, 2), and Marks equates Kino with the good. This equation is hardly borne out by a careful reading of the novel. As the story develops, Kino must learn what is good; he is a pilgrim in search of values. Juana is a constant. Though Kino must learn of the evil that greed engenders, Juana is instinctively aware that the pearl is a thing of bad luck. Her values never change. She is, from beginning to end, devoted to the preservation of her loved ones, man and child.

In his comment on the novelette, Warren French observes that Steinbeck changed the original legend on which *The Pearl* is based to include Juana.[16] The anonymous boy in the legend, first published by Steinbeck in *The Log from the Sea of Cortez*, is unmarried. In fact, one of the things he wants to spend his money on is women. However, French does not explore the implications of Steinbeck's alterations. If all Steinbeck had wished to transmit through his novelette was the idea that greed and frustration are all that result from material gain, then he would not have needed to add a courageous and enduring woman to his cast of characters. None of the characters in the original version are exemplars of positive values. Besides buying himself many women, the Indian fisherboy wants to use the money from the pearl's sale to allow him to loaf, get drunk, and buy his way into heaven. By making the boy into a married man, and adding a woman and a child, Steinbeck enlarges the scope of the message. The negative results affect more people. Kino loses not only the pearl, but the baby (his posterity) is killed, and his boat (his livelihood) is smashed. In Steinbeck's revision of the story, the outcome is seemingly more pessimistic than in the original. What relieves the dark future and differentiates Steinbeck's message from the cynical message of the original is the character of Juana. Though Kino loses the pearl, he retains her loyalty and devotion. Though the baby is dead, the presence of Juana presages future children.

Harry Morris subjects *The Pearl* to a thorough and careful scrutiny, but though he analyzes the importance of Coyotito, he barely mentions Juana.[17] Neither Gray nor O'Connor finds her character worthy of note. Considering the importance of her function in the plot, and the care with which Steinbeck develops her positive qualities, this is a lamentable oversight on the part of discerning critics. Sandra Beatty, on the other hand, describes Juana as both dynamic and memorable, one endowed with a distinctly female wisdom.[18]

Steinbeck obviously had the image of a very good and very strong woman in mind when he created Juana. Conceivably she could have been characterized as a carbon copy of Kino, mirroring his moods and desires much like some of Hemingway's submissive heroines, or she could have been portrayed similarly to the avaricious wife in the fairy tale "The Fisherman and His Wife."[19] But Juana is neither docile nor greedy. Her positive characteristics are carefully delineated. She is clearly another example of Steinbeck's indestructible women.

Besides those few characteristics which distinguish her as an individual woman, and Steinbeck did particularize her enough to give her a name, not a necessity in a parable, Juana also embodies many of the nurturing qualities traditionally associated with woman. Those qualities are stressed through the imagery that depicts Juana as the Great Mother, always on guard to protect her own. One of the ways Steinbeck imparts this idea is in his description of Juana's eternal watchfulness. "Juana's eyes were open too. Kino could never remember seeing them closed when he awakened. Her dark eyes made little deflected stars. She was looking at him as she was always looking at him when he awakened" (P, 3). Later in the novelette, when they are being pursued, Juana guards Kino's sleep.

Juana's devotion to the family is concretized in the music Kino hears in her presence and in the three-note ancient song she sings. The song's message is "this is safety, this is warmth, this is the *whole*" (P, 6). When that safety is threatened, Juana's reaction sounds the echo of that family song in Kino's perception. "And Kino saw her determination and the music of the family sounded in his head with a steely tone" (P, 13). It is Juana's determination that goads Kino into going for the doctor when the doctor has refused to respond to their call for him.

Throughout the fable Juana is depicted as the more effectual of the two. When the baby is bitten, it is Juana who sucks out the poison. "Kino hovered, he was helpless, he was in the way"(P, 11). When the doctor will not come, it is Juana who practically wills the finding of the pearl that insures the doctor's attendance. Juana's is a magic of intense will, "her face set, rigid, and her muscles hard to force the luck, to tear the luck out of the gods' hands, for she needed the luck for the swollen shoulder of Coyotito." Ironically, although she accomplishes the forcing of the luck, it turns out to be bad luck that she brings upon them. Coyotito is saved by her quick action in sucking out the venom, not by the doctor, and possession of the pearl leads eventually to his death.

Steinbeck's characterization of Juana is unremittingly noble. She is the epitome of endurance and devotion. This devotion, however, is not of the unquestioning doglike or servile type. When Juana's better judgment decides that the pearl will only bring disaster, she defies Kino and tries to throw it away. Her reward is a beating. Defeated in her attempt to dispose of the pearl, she resigns herself to standing by Kino. "Juana, in her woman's soul, knew that the mountain would stand while the man broke himself, that the sea would surge while the man drowned in it" (P, 85). Both the mountain and the sea are traditional symbols for the archetypal feminine and like the mountain, Juana endures though Kino's actions break him and result in the death of Coyotito. That Steinbeck is generalizing about the nature of woman is made clear: "Sometimes the quality of woman, the reason, the caution, the sense of preservation, could cut through Kino's manness and save them all" (P, 85). The qualities of women that will save the world, in Steinbeck's perception, from the impetuous shortsighted manness, are those same qualities that make of woman a survivor, her indestructibility.

But Juana does more than just survive—she is a source of strength. When Kino confronts the pearl buyers, she backs him up. "Kino was silent and watchful. He felt a little tugging at his back, and he turned and looked in Juana's eyes, and when he looked away he had renewed strength" (P, 70). When his determination flags, she encourages him. When the situation gets dangerous, she will not leave him, though he tries to make her go. "He looked then for weakness in her face, for fear or irresolution, and there was none. Her eyes were very bright. He shrugged his shoulders helplessly then, but he had taken strength from her" (P, 106). But Juana's most incredible show of strength and wisdom comes at the end of the fable when her worst dread has been realized. It is then that she acts like Ma and like Pilar and allows her man to regain his sense of dignity. Kino knows that Juana was right and therefore gives her the pearl to throw back into the sea; rather than throw the pearl back herself, she has the sensitivity to give it to Kino so that he can do it himself.

Juana combines all the best qualities of wife and mother. But Steinbeck does not portray her as traditionally feminine in a submissive or weak way. She is loyal and strong, protective, but not dominating. Her relationship with her husband is so elemental that the need for speech is eliminated. "They had spoken once, but there is not need for speech, if it is only a habit anyway, Kino sighed with satisfaction—and that was conversation" (P, 9). The lack of verbalization, however, does not indicate a lack of knowledge or communication. Kino is very much aware of Juana's admirable qualities: "Kino had wondered often at the iron in his patient, fragile wife. She, who was obedient and respectful and cheerful and patient, she could arch her back in child pain with hardly a cry. She could stand fatigue and hunger almost better than Kino himself. In the canoe she was like a strong man" (P, 12). Steinbeck does not show any weak or ugly traits in Juana's personality.

But for all of her positive characteristics, Juana remains a flat character. As a representative of womankind, she is nurturing and indestructible. As an individual, one woman, wife to Kino, mother to Coyotito, her personality never takes shape. But then, neither does Kino's, even though we are shown the negative aspects of his character. Of course, the parable style practically precludes realistic or psychologically detailed character studies. Juana is, as the narrator makes clear, *woman*. She is mother, she is wife, but she is also teacher. Her function in the novelette is much like that of the Code Hero in a number of Hemingway stories. She knows the values. Kino must learn them. Because she does, and because she remains steadfast, loyal, and committed to family, the end of the novel has an optimistic cast. The price has been high, but Kino and Juana are together and more children are possible in the future.

Ma Joad and Juana are important because they are major characters in major works, works that have been generally applauded by the critics. A cursory reading of all of Steinbeck's novels, however, will reveal that there are not many other important female characters in them. In fact, as I have pointed out in another study, there is a singular scarcity of women in Steinbeck's fiction.[20] The world, according to Steinbeck, whose works have often been lauded for their scientific objectivity, is strangely only about one-fourth female. The reasons for this peculiar skewing of reality are not clear. Steinbeck's life was full of significant female relationships. Though he was the only boy in a family of four, the families he usually depicts are predominantly masculine. In the Joad family, Ruthie and Rose of Sharon are outnumbered by their brothers. In many of his families there are no sisters. His focus instead is on the relationship between brothers. The Trask family in *East of Eden* is male for two generations as Steinbeck explores the implications of the Cain and Abel paradigm. The Wayne family of *To a God Unknown* is a family of brothers. If Steinbeck's focus is not on biological brothers, he often pictures other instances of close male bonding. Danny and Pilon of *Tortilla Flat,* George and Lennie in *Of Mice and Men,* and Mac and Jim of *In Dubious Battle* are three examples that come easily to mind.

Much has been made of Steinbeck's friendship with Ed Ricketts and a number of critics have explored the effect of that relationship on Steinbeck's writing. Steinbeck modeled a number of his characters either directly after Ricketts or gave them aspects of Ricketts's personality. The most obvious example is Doc in *Cannery Row,* the novel which is dedicated to Ricketts. In others of his works, Steinbeck expounds biological theories about humanity which were ideas he shared with Ricketts; Ricketts was a marine biologist and Steinbeck had a lifelong interest in the subject. The relationship also produced publications of a nonfictional character. *Sea of Cortez: A Leisurely Journal of Travel and Research* is a collaboration of the two men which is both a narrative of the trip and a highly technical catalogue of the specimens they collected. The work that they did together is well documented.[21] Of course, *Sea of Cortez* has a strong fictional aspect. The dramatic narratives of the crew's adventures are remarkable vignettes, spiced with the famed Steinbeckian humor.[22] It might be significant that though Steinbeck's wife Carol was on the trip, her presence is expunged from the book. Ricketts's influence on Steinbeck was considerable; various writers have contended that Ricketts's death marked the beginning of the decline of Steinbeck's literary power.[23]

While there is no denying the importance of Ricketts in Steinbeck's life, what Steinbeck ignored in his fiction and what many writers have since ignored in their tracing of influences on Steinbeck is the number of important women who helped shape and direct his writing career. Jackson Benson's biography goes far in correcting this deficiency. As Benson points out, Steinbeck was a man who needed to be married, who was dependent on women.[24] Carol Henning Steinbeck's contribution to her husband's writing is detailed by Benson and will be explicated further when Gene Detro's authorized biography of Carol appears.[25]

That both Hemingway and Steinbeck are writers whose fictional worlds are one-sidedly masculine is undeniable. The proof is there in terms of numbers of male and female characters; the proof is there in terms of theme and plot patterns. Steinbeck like Hemingway chooses to focus on the male quest and on male companionship.[26] Hemingway's masculine absorption reduces many of his women to negative or positive funtionaries. Steinbeck's masculine bent has in many cases practically reduced them out of existence.

Given our knowledge of the way Steinbeck readjusted his fictional world to omit the women who populated his real world, the significance of those women he chooses to portray is intensified. Besides Ma Joad and Juana, two major characters of heroic proportions, there are other female characters in both the short stories and the novels, who, while not as admirable as the aforementioned women, still serve as exemplars of that indestructible quality in women that Steinbeck found, if not admirable, then at least awe-inspiring. While one hesitates to suggest simplistic categories for a writer as variable as Steinbeck, most of his indestructible women are either mothers or whores.

The mothers outnumber the whores, but the whores definitely have a positive place in the rolls of Steinbeck's indestructible females. For the most part their characterization is hopelessly romantic. Steinbeck is a devoted subscriber to the myth of the whore with a heart of gold. To that description he adds a spine of steel. Cathy Ames Trask is a notable exception to his coterie of "happy hookers."[27] But *East of Eden* comes late in Steinbeck's development as a writer.

The Lopez sisters in one of Steinbeck's earliest works, *The Pastures of Heaven,* are two of his most sentimentally drawn prostitutes. Steinbeck deals whimsically with their entrance into the profession. They are left penniless and having no way to earn a living, they open a small Spanish restaurant. To encourage business Rosa gives herself to a man who has bought three enchiladas. This then becomes the pattern for both sisters. Happily rationalizing their situation, they accept money only for the cooking and pray for forgiveness to the Mother Virgin each time they "encourage" the customers. Rosa and Maria are plump, merry, and proud women with the sense to knowingly deceive themselves since it facilitates survival. The true test of their indomitability, however, comes when they can no longer run their "restaurant." Rather than starve, they give up the restaurant and move to San Francisco to become professional prostitutes. What Steinbeck seems to be saying is that the two women have the strength to deceive themselves when they can, thus making their prostitution more palatable, but they also face up to harsh reality when they must. Men, in Steinbeck's stories, often collapse when they have to discard their illusions. Adaptability is one of the characteristics that most of his indestructible women, like the Lopez sisters, share. In that way Steinbeck's characterization implies a Darwinian precedent, in keeping with his biological view of humanity.

The story of the Lopez sisters is but one episode among many in *The Pastures of Heaven*. The story of Suzy, the gutsy little hustler, is at the core of *Sweet Thursday*. Its musical comedy plot (it was later turned into just that) is the love story of Suzy and Doc, who makes a return appearance after *Cannery Row*. Steinbeck's characterization of Suzy reads like a response to the cliche question, "What's a nice girl like you doing in a place like this?" To distinguish Suzy from the other prostitutes, Steinbeck has both Joseph and Mary, the Patron, and Fauna, the Madame of the Bear Flag, recognize that she is more than the ordinary hustler. Both comment on her strength and both acknowledge her warmth and special qualities.

On the literal level, Suzy shows her indestructibility in that through sheer determination and will she leaves her profession and builds herself a respectable existence in an old boiler in order to be what she feels Doc would want in a woman. On a symbolic level, the reader is given certain clues that suggest that Suzy represents not only womanhood but all the downtrodden of society. To Joe Elegant, the would-be author, Suzy is "the mass." "I'm the mass, huh? I guess you got something there" (ST, 83), she replies to his classification. Doc also generalizes from her behavior. When he sees Suzy's living conditions in the boiler he exclaims, "My God, what a brave thing is the human!" (ST, 248).

Throughout the novel, Suzy's indomitable characteristics are stressed. She comes from a broken home, a broken marriage, she loses her expected child, she is humiliated and rejected by Doc, and still she has the courage and fortitude to persevere. When Doc finally realizes his need and desire for her, he stops to analyze the special quality in her that he so admires, her indestructibility. He compares her to Bach, finding her indomitability even greater than Bach's as she had more to overcome than he did. As Doc explains:

> Bach fought savagely.... He was not defeated.... Old Bach had his talent and his family and his friends. Everyone has something. And what has Suzy got? Absolutely nothing in the world but guts. She's taken on an atomic world with a slingshot, and, by God she's going to win! If she doesn't win there's no point in living any more. (ST, 245-46)

Suzy does win. And symbolically all humanity wins through her since she is "the mass." But while she is the mass, Steinbeck is careful to delineate the decidedly female cast of her indomitable qualities. On the brink of her victory she begins behaving in a shy and girlish manner like a traditionally brought up woman rather than a reformed prostitute. Lest we be fooled by Suzy's reversal, the narrator assures us, "as anybody knows, there is nothing more indestructible and deadly than a shy young girl" (ST, 268).

Suzy's portrayal is so unabashedly romantic that she is given liberties accorded few women in Steinbeck's works. She gets to move from one category to another. She begins the novel as a whore, but by the end of the novel, as she rides off into the future with Doc, motherhood is a distinct possibility. Her direction is a positive one, for motherhood is the most telling constant in Steinbeck's characterization of the indestructible woman. Other indestructible mothers, along with Juana and Ma Joad, are Mordeen in *Burning Bright*, Mama Torres in "Flight," Rama in *To a God Unknown* and several women in *Pastures of Heaven*.

Helen Van Deveter, Katherine Wicks, and Alicia Whiteside of *Pastures of Heaven* illustrate three diverse and yet distinctly similar aspects of the indestructible maternal figure as drawn by Steinbeck. All have great difficulties to overcome. For Helen Van Deveter, the problems seem to be partially self-induced although there are certainly also externally caused problems. The narrator tells us that a strong awareness of tragedy has run through Helen's life. When she was 15 her Persian kitten was poisoned. Her father died soon after. When she married, she lost her husband in a freak hunting accident; he tripped and shot himself. Her daughter, born six months later, was never physically well and is mentally disturbed. None of the above is of Helen's doing, but her martyrlike reaction to her tragedies causes her doctor to comment, "It seems to me you force hardships upon yourself" (PH, 50). Helen's rationale for her behavior reads like a credo for the indestructible woman: "We take what is given us. I can endure, I am sure of that, and I am proud of it. No amount of tragedy can break down my endurance" (PH, 50–51). Helen proves true to her word when tested. Extreme circumstances lead her to believe she must kill her own demented child.

The reader does not admire Helen. Steinbeck shows us that in the case of her daughter, the martyrdom is unnecessary. Helen's doctor suggests several times that the daughter would be better off in a mental institution. However, Helen gains strength from adversity. Enduring the tragedy of the life she chooses with her daughter sustains her. The daughter shrieks, breaks windows and furniture, slits pillows, and generally makes life miserable for Helen. At times it seems Helen might succumb. "For a moment the dumb endurance had nearly broken, but instantly it settled back more strongly than ever, and the shrieks from Hilda's room had no effect" (PH, 55).

Helen, like others of Steinbeck's indestructible women, can also adapt to change. She can live with the misery of her daughter or without it. After she has killed Hilda she continues to bear up. The doctor, who comes to help her through the horrors of the inquest in which the murder is ruled a suicide, sees that Helen is not afraid. "In her severe, her almost savage mourning, she looked as enduring as a sea-washed stone" (PH, 63). The doctor hopes that the death of the child will free Helen to live a more normal life. Helen, it seems, prefers martyrdom. "I know now. By this time I know what my life expects of me.... And I have the strength to endure, Doctor. Don't you worry about me" (PH, 64).

Whereas Steinbeck depicts Helen as a person whose indestructibility practically invites disasters, just so she can have the masochistic pleasure of bearing them, in his characterization of Alicia Whiteside he shows a woman whose endurance is admirable. She shares the dynastic dreams of her husband and is anxious to play her role in the perpetuation of the generations, but her first birth nearly kills her and the doctor tells Richard Whiteside, "Have another child and you won't have any wife" (PH, 161). Nevertheless, Alicia insists on trying to have another child. Richard assents, thinking, "It's the grain of deity in women. . . . Nature has planted this sure knowledge in women in order that the race may increase" (PH, 163). Unfortunately, Alicia has a very high price to pay for her devotion to the increase of the race. She goes through a horrible confinement and although she does not die, she becomes an invalid. The doctor comments, "Your wife isn't dead, Heaven only knows why. She's gone through enough to kill a squad of soldiers. These weak women. They have the vitality of monsters" (PH, 164).

Alicia retains a goddesslike position in the household. She is carried about and ministered to like an idol. Her husband defers to her superior wisdom—"And Richard knew that it was a greater knowledge than his" (PH, 165). The neighborhood children speak softly and tiptoe in her home. When her son John prepares to marry, his fiancée must first submit to a thorough interrogation by Alicia. Once Alicia is secure in the knowledge that the dynasty will be perpetuated by her new daughter-in-law, she feels free to die. Her husband, who was always healthy, has died years before. He had told Alicia, "Make John realize he must keep us going. I want to survive in the generations" (PH, 166). Alicia, who is frail and sickly, hangs on to fulfill her husband's wish. Such is her strength.

Still a third indomitable woman in *Pastures of Heaven* is Katherine Wicks. Katherine is the embodiment of the Earth Mother. In her descriptions, Steinbeck stresses her connections to nature: "She had the firm freshness of a new weed, and the bridling vigour of a young mare" (PH, 18). After marriage she is compared to a flower that has received pollen. Through most of the section of the novel dealing with the Wicks family, Katherine is not portrayed as a particularly romantic figure. Notwithstanding her earlier description, her relationship with her husband is cold and businesslike; he treats her not like another human being, but like one of his workhorses.

The full significance of Helen's earth mother qualities is not understood until a time of crisis. When she must become woman the nurturer, when her husband is broken and defeated, she reaches the apex of her strength. Responding to what Steinbeck describes as a warm genius which suffuses her being, Helen becomes the Great Mother. She takes her husband, who has always been a pillar of stength, and cradles his head in her lap: "Katherine stroked his head gently and the great genius continued to grow in her. She felt larger than the world. The whole world was in her lap and she comforted it. Pity seemed to make her huge in stature. Her soothing breast yearned toward the woe of the world" (PH, 34). Helen is aware of her destiny at this moment. She takes on the mantle of the eternal nourishing mother. Rather than becoming strong herself, however, she feeds her strength into her husband, just as a mother's nourishment is drained off by her nursing child. Katherine's power is even described in terms that might suggest a mother's milk. "Suddenly the genius in Katherine became power and the power gushed in her body and flooded her" (PH, 34).

The narrator tells us that Katherine has always been aware that she had this power deep within her. "She had known she could do this. As she sat there the knowledge of her power had been born in her, and she knew that all her life was directed at this one moment. In this moment she was a goddess, a singer of destiny" (PH, 34). Like many of her indestructible sisters, Helen's main function is not to do, but to be the source from which men gain the strength to act. When Shark's vitality has been restored, he forgets about Katherine. The reader is sure, however, that Katherine will be there, a source of strength if her man should need her again.

Pastures of Heaven is in the form of a novel, but it is actually a series of short stories that share the same setting, and have the connecting link of the deleterious effect on various individuals of their interaction with members of the Munroe family. None of the characters is very fully developed. Many of the women, however, are very strong and Steinbeck uses a number of them to illustrate the indestructibility of the female.

One of the strongest examples of female endurance in Steinbeck's short stories is Mama Torres in "Flight." Mama Torres has suffered much. She struggles to eke out a meager living from the barren land and stingy sea. Steinbeck describes her as "a lean, dry woman with ancient eyes" (LV, 45). She has been the sole support of her family since the day, 10 years earlier, when "her husband tripped over a stone and fell full length on a rattlesnake" (LV, 45). Mama Torres is resigned to her hard lot. She accepts what comes. The big test of her ability to endure comes when her eldest child Pepe reaches manhood, or thinks he has. Mama Torres dreads the day, but she must allow her boy-child to become a man even though it is extremely painful for her. With patience she views his typically boyish pastime, throwing a knife. She has a woman's scorn for this masculine activity, but she is aware of its significance in Pepe's development: "Yes thou art a man, my poor little Pepe; thou art a man. I have seen it coming on thee, I have watched you throwing the knife into the post, and I have been afraid" (LV, 52). Inevitably, as Mama has feared, this prelude to aggressive masculine behavior leads to the real thing. A man challenges Pepe's honor and Pepe kills him with a knife.

Pepe's aggression and knife-throwing are expected masculine behavior. Pepe identifies them with manhood. As he explains, "I am a man now, Mama. The man said names to me I could not allow" (LV, 52). What manhood has to offer Pepe is death, but first he participates in another traditional masculine ritual, the hunt.

Mama Torres's nourishing behavior and endurance identify her with womanhood. She summons the necessary strength to send her firstborn to an unknown destiny. As always, she provides for his basic needs, giving him food, water, blankets, and a gun. She does what has to be done. Pepe looks for a crack in her invulnerability: "Pepe turned back to Mama. He seemed to look for a little softness, a little weakness in her. His eyes were searching, but Mama's face remained fierce. 'Go now,' she said. 'Do not wait to be caught here like a chicken'" (LV, 54). Mama Torres is controlled enough not to break in Pepe's presence. She plays the role, much like Ma Joad and others of Steinbeck's indestructible women, of inspiring strength in those who look to her. Only when Pepe is gone does Mama finally break down and show her great unhappiness. She wails and mourns, sure that Pepe will be killed, and then goes into the house. The reader does not see her again. The rest of the story is devoted to Pepe's flight and eventual death. Nevertheless, the implication is clear. Mama will go on as she always has, nourishing and sustaining the next generation, male and female alike, personified in Rosy and Emilio, her remaining children. Rosy's extrasensory perception hints that when her time comes she will possess the same strength and womanly wisdom as her mother.

Steinbeck's use of the imagery that connects woman and the earth began early. Perhaps the work in which it is most evident is *To a God Unknown*. Though later works also utilize the woman/earth symbology, in this early work the identification is heavy-handedly blatant. To Joseph Wayne, the protagonist, the earth and woman are one. He feels a similar passion for both, hungering to possess the land as one might possess a woman. When he does reach the land he will claim as his own, he consummates the possession with a symbolic intercourse.

> He stamped his feet into the soft earth. Then the exultance grew to a sharp pain of desire that ran through his body in a hot river. He flung himself face downward on the grass and pressed his cheek against the wet stems. His fingers gripped the wet grass and tore it out, and gripped again. His thigh beat heavily on the earth. (TGU, 8)

The significance of his behavior is not lost on Joseph. He is aware that for the moment the land had been his wife.

Joseph is obsessed with fecundity. "He willed that all things about him must grow, grow quickly, conceive and multiply. The hopeless sin was barrenness, a sin intolerable and unforgivable" (TGU, 22). The narrator explains Joseph's adoration of the bitch "swollen with puppies" and the cow "fat with calf" as "the heritage of a race which for a million years has sucked at the breasts of the soil and co-habited with the earth" (TGU, 22). The woman-is-earth imagery in this metaphor is obvious. It is a connection which was particularly strong in the mind-set of those explorers and pioneers who first settled our country.[28]

In *To a God Unknown* the most obvious earth mother figure is Rama, Joseph's sister-in-law. She is the repository of all the virtues Steinbeck associated with indestructible women. On the farm she acts as the matriarch, exerting a goddesslike authority over all within her domain. Her characterization stresses her maternal and forceful qualities. She is "strong" and "full-breasted." She presides at births as a "good and efficient midwife," and then because her authority extends beyond the birth she "automatically took charge of all children who came near her" (TGU, 20). All the children recognize her authority, and that authority derives from her connection to the Eternal Feminine. Rama represents an everlasting standard, "for the laws of Rama never changed." Goddesslike Rama metes out reward and punishment. "Her praise could be as delicate and sharp as her punishment was terrible" (TGU, 20). As representative of the eternal maternal, Rama has little patience with the temporal concerns of men. "She was nearly always contemptuous of everything men thought or did" (TGU, 19). She knows that her function is the significant one, "much more important than the things men did." In this she is much like Faulkner's Granny Rosa Millard and Miss Jenny DuPre; her priorities are set by her role as preserver of the species. Demeter-like she reproduces herself; Rama has three daughters.

Throughout the novel Rama works as a positive and life-sustaining force. She is the midwife to Joseph and Elizabeth's baby and when Elizabeth dies, it is Rama who takes the baby to raise. Rama also heals Joseph's pain after Elizabeth's death. Acting in her incarnation as the Great Mother, Rama comes to Joseph as healer and surrogate mate. He cannot eat or sleep. Rama knows that he has to be shaken out of his unwholesome state. She mates with him and theirs is a violent and explosive lovemaking. In a rituallike incantation she takes his pain into herself. "The long deep river of sorrow is diverted and sucked into me..." (TGU, 136). Having eased his pain and fulfilled his need, she leaves with the proclamation, "You are complete again" (TGU, 136). Joseph falls into a deep, healing sleep. It never happens again. Because of Rama's special qualities, she is not judged by conventional standards. There is no suggestion of any moral condemnation of this adulterous act, either through the guilt of the characters or narrative implication.

Nevertheless, despite all of Rama's and Joseph's efforts, the situation in the valley does not improve. Life begins to depart the valley, but Joseph refuses to leave. In the end he slits his wrists and sacrifices himself to bring rain to the parched land. If there is any hope for the future of the Wayne family, it is embodied in Rama, who takes her own children and Joseph's child to care for and raise.

To a God Unknown was an early work; *Burning Bright* was written some 20 years later. Steinbeck's reverence for female fecundity is undiminished. Peter Lisca explains this as part of Steinbeck's biological image of humanity.

In many species of insects and some vertebrates the female destroys the male after copulation. Steinbeck must have linked such an incident into his great biological chain of being, perhaps as evidence of the ubiquitous female drive to procreate and protect at all cost her offspring.[29]

Mordeen, the mother figure in this play/novel, uses Victor as a stud to provide a child for her sterile husband, Joe Saul. When the stud tries to assert his paternal rights, he is killed, needlessly, as Joe Saul finds out he is sterile anyway. Steinbeck seems to accept that behavior. There is no implicit or explicit moral censure of Mordeen's actions. The message would seem to be that reproduction has a sanctity of its own. Mordeen commits adultery and murder, but motherhood puts her beyond the moral pale. Friend Ed's description of Mordeen's "holy" act implies as much: "She is giving you a child—yours—to be your own. Her love for you is so great that she could do a thing that was strange and foul to her and yet not be dirtied by it" (BB, 147–48). At the end of the novel Mordeen gives birth to the baby who is a result of her relationship with Victor. Joe Saul, a good man and spokesperson for the biological credo, proclaims: "I thought they [his own features] were worth preserving because they were mine. It is not so. It is the race, the species must go staggering on. . . . The baby is alive. This is the only important thing" (BB, 157). Mordeen, whose greater wisdom goes beyond mere ethical and moral concerns, is like a pagan mother goddess. Her fertility is worshipped. An indestructible woman, she endures, not subject to temporal laws, secure in her role as perpetuator of the species.

By the end of the 1940s Steinbeck was ready to attempt another big book, a book with the rather ambitious purpose of not only telling the story of his family but of "the whole nasty bloody lovely history of the world."[30] In that story women play a significant role. Cathy/Kate, who is both Terrible Mother and Duplicitous Eve in one, dominates most of the novel. Hers is the character who fascinates readers; she is the character about whom the plot of fraternal rivalry revolves. The major female figure in this generational saga is a monster, perhaps the most vituperative villainess in American fiction. She occupies both of the categories Steinbeck reserves for women; she is both a mother and a whore. But, contrary to his usual sentimentalization of these roles, Steinbeck shows Cathy as a malevolent mother, one who tries to abort and then abandons her children. She is also a far cry from his usual whore with a heart of gold.

The myth that underlies *East of Eden* is the Cain and Abel story, the archetype for sibling rivalry and fratricide. Steinbeck identifies himself and all of us, since we are all the children of Cain, with Cal, the Cain figure who indirectly causes the death of his brother. Cal must learn about his nature and about his choices in life. The operative theme is the concept of "timshel," God's injunction to Cain which either commands him to triumph over evil or gives him the choice to do so. Caleb chooses redemption, but he does not do it alone. He is strongly supported by Abra, one of Steinbeck's most positively depicted women. *East of Eden* is a novel with an optimistic conclusion and Abra is instrumental in that outcome.

Steinbeck's purpose in creating the character of Abra is in no way ambiguous. He tells us in *Journal of a Novel* that he intends for her to represent "the strong female principle of good." She is to be "a fighter and an effective human being."[31] Steinbeck succeeds admirably. Abra is an appealing character, good and yet realistically human. Steinbeck tells us in his narrator's commentary that there is only one story in the world and that that is the "never-ending contest in ourselves of good and evil" (EE, 477). Abra, who is very much aware of the bad in herself, consciously chooses the good. Not only does she choose a positive role for herself, but she encourages Cal in that direction also. When he would hide from the terrible reality of his actions and his father's illness by returning to the womblike security of the "sweetly protected and warm and safe" envelopment of the willow tree, she forces him home instead.[32]

Abra's good judgment is inherent. Even as a little girl she is described as having "wisdom and sweetness in her expression." When she and Aron are both children, she mothers him and treats him with "condescending wisdom" (EE, 486–87). In their play she wants to pretend to be his wife, but Aron wants her to be the mother he never had, a role she slips into easily. She coos at Aron, "Come, my baby, put your head in Mother's lap" (EE, 488). Lee, the novel's resident sage, understands her inherent maturity when he calls the teenaged Abra "a good woman—a real woman." Cal counters that she is a girl, but Lee corrects him. "No. ... A few are women from the moment they're born. Abra has the loveliness of woman, and the courage—and the strength—and the wisdom" (EE, 659).

In his description of Abra, Steinbeck makes observations about women's ability to focus on the larger picture, the eternal rather than temporal view, which are similar to some of Faulkner's. When Aron plunges into a religious fervor, we are told Abra's reaction by the narrator: "Her feminine mind knew that such things were necessary but unimportant" (EE, 516). When Aron chooses celibacy, "Abra in her wisdom agreed with him, feeling and hoping that this phase would pass" (EE, 517). Abra is able to take the long view, to see beyond the exigencies of the moment at the tender age of 14, a rare feat.

If the reader is to accept Steinbeck's contemporary rendering of the Cain and Abel myth as representative of the "whole nasty bloody lovely history of the world," then Abra as a second Eve is also a prototype for the feminine. The adjective that Steinbeck uses most often to characterize her is strong. Besides the descriptions of her already cited, the narrator also pictures her as "straight, strong, fine-breasted" (EE, 564), and in another instance her "strength and goodness" and "warmth" are specified. She is womanly, but it is a womanliness of "bold muscular strength" (565).

Abra does not shrink from her womanly role. She rejects Aron's desire to idealize her, to turn her into a "Goddess-Virgin." She does not want to be an ethereal being, the angel woman of Aron's fantasies (EE, 567). She wants to be a sexual being, a biological mother in a relationship with a man who sees her as a flesh and blood human being rather than one who has created his own version of her. The prognosis for her future is a good one. In the final scene of the novel Lee is trying to communicate to Adam the importance of his forgiving Cal and giving him his blessing. He brings Cal and Abra into the room with him and points out to Adam that Cal's and Abra's children "will be the only remnant left of you" (EE, 599). With great effort Adam provides that blessing by uttering the reinforcing word "timshel," the word that communicates to Cal that he can choose to triumph over the sin he has committed and live a good and full life with Abra.

5

Some Conclusions

Dilsey, Miss Habersham, Dewey Dell; Lady Brett, Pilar, Renata; Ma Joad, Suzy, Mordeen—characters so physically and psychologically diverse that one is hard put to discover any linking characteristic save for the fact that they are all female. And yet, as this study has illustrated, each of these women, besides whatever other function she performs in her creator's plot, also serves as the embodiment of an attitude about women that duplicates itself in works otherwise diverse and individual. This attitude suggests that there is something in the essential nature of woman, something which strengthens her, some psychic cushioning which, like the subcutaneous layer of fat that distinguishes the female anatomy from that of the male, provides a natural insulation which better equips woman for survival.

Recent physiological studies verify the fact that when it comes to sports which require stamina rather than speed or strength, women are indeed better equipped biologically than men. Women cannot run as fast, but they are in better physical shape at the end of a marathon than the men who fall prostrate over the finish line. Women are the record-breakers in channel swims and long-distance swimming races though they cannot compete with men in short speed races. In our generation women outlive men. But Faulkner, Hemingway, and Steinbeck were not privy to the recent studies about comparative male and female physiology; their concepts about female biology were formed way before women were even allowed to actively participate in such arduous competitions as the Olympics. There are no Diana Nyads or Joan Benoits in their works. None of the women they portray is an athlete. And yet, to play upon the metaphor, Faulkner, Hemingway, and Steinbeck often portray women as the marathoners of our society, the ones who can last through the rigors of the long and demanding race. Their indestructible women exhibit a channel swimmer's stamina as they navigate the tumultuous seas of life.

These writers, however scientifically objective they may have attempted to be, did not draw their female portraitures from physiological premises. Their recognition of female stamina and endurance developed in each as a result of his singular vision of the truths of human existence. These truths for them, as for everyone, derive from the interrelationship between personal experiences and the cultural myths that permeate society.

The contemporary reader must be reminded that each of these writers was, in his own way, a pioneer in overcoming taboos about what it was permissible to portray, particularly in matters of sexuality or physicality. Students of today are amazed when they learn that such books as *The Grapes of Wrath*, *A Farewell to Arms*, and *Sanctuary* were banned from high school libraries. Even the authors' own families were appalled by what they considered their sons' breaches of decorum. Hemingway's mother thought *The Sun Also Rises* was a dirty book. Faulkner's father once chastised a University of Mississippi coed when he caught her carrying a copy of *Sanctuary* on campus.

Still, as avant-garde as they were for their times in their portrayal of women and sexuality, they are still also children of their age. All three men were born within five years of each other and their deaths all fall within the same decade:

> William Faulkner (1897–1962)
> Ernest Hemingway (1898–1961)
> John Steinbeck (1902–1968)

They produced the bulk of their important works in the 1920s, 1930s, and 1940s. And though what they may have depicted about women and sexuality flew in the face of early-twentieth-century conventionality, read in the 1980s, their works reflect their cultural and historical limitations.

The early twentieth century was a period of upheaval and transition in the role of women. During the first two decades of the century, the move for suffrage challenged the universal denial of voting rights. With the enactment of the Nineteenth Amendment, the federal government legally declared that women were equal to men and Negroes, who had been nominally enfranchised by the Fourteenth Amendment. The actualization of this radical idea, however, came after the formative years of Faulkner, Hemingway, and Steinbeck. By the time of the Nineteenth Amendment, they had long since formed their initial conceptions of male and female roles in society and in interpersonal relationships. These early conceptions can be intellectually replaced, but they remain imbedded in the psyche. Their emotional residue is never totally vanquished. While Faulkner, Hemingway, and Steinbeck were in many ways rebels against conventional morality about sexuality, a certain ambiguity toward "liberated" women is reflected in their works. Even as she is resurrected in *Requiem for a Nun*, Temple Drake is far from an appealing person. Hemingway's depiction of the destruction wrought by Brett Ashley, who dresses like and drinks like a man, suggests that though she is attractive and exhibits her own kind of courage and indestructibility, men who come in contact with her do not fare well. Steinbeck was unable to face the reality of self-sustaining, independent women in nontraditional roles in his fiction. Though his professors, agents, and sometimes the models for his labor organizers were women, traditional female occupations such as mothering, teaching school, and prostitution are the only employments he allowed his fictional women.[1]

Still, each of these writers attempts in the occasional short story and sometimes through characters in novels to portray if not the new woman at least the free-spirited woman and her difficulties vis-à-vis the constraints of conventional gender roles. Linda Snopes is Faulkner's most successful "new woman" though many readers have pointed out that he found it necessary to wound her and mutilate her voice, leaving her deaf and "quacking." Steinbeck's portrayal of Elisa in "The Chrysanthemums" illustrates his ability to understand the problems of a woman of energy and ability, isolated from other women and told by her society and the peddler that her desires for freedom and adventure "ain't the right kind of life for a woman." Hemingway's early sensitivity to woman's difficulty in coping with new freedoms is expressed in his understanding of the boyishly coiffed young wife's desire to grow long hair and sit at her own table set with silver and candles in "Cat in the Rain."

A sociological approach, one that focuses on the problems of individuals in contemporary society, yields some insights. Each of these men did address political issues of their times through their fiction: Faulkner, race relations; Hemingway, war; Steinbeck, migrant workers. In each case, as political situations change, the relevance of that aspect of their works can be reevaluated. Faulkner, who was considered a traitor by conservative Southerners because of his sympathy for blacks, lived to be called a racist. Hemingway's portrayal of men and women during wartime, their losses, individual compromises, and the heavy toll we all pay is as revealing today as it was for the wars he wrote about. The problem of migrant workers is still with us for all the political furor raised by *The Grapes of Wrath*. The works of these writers continue to be relevant to readers today because they can be read not only for what they tell us of their times but also for the timelessness of their themes. Faced with the richness and depth of the works of these three writers, the critic who attempts to posit answers based in only one critical approach will surely be limited to one layer of the work.

The works of Frazer had burst on the literary scene in the early part of this century and these three writers were aware not only of his work, but also of the works of other theorists on the subjects of myth and archetype. Faulkner's awareness of and use of Frazer is heavily documented. Faulkner not only used those myths he read in Frazer and the Bible, but found his literary voice in the creation of his own mythic kingdom. His interweaving of any number of mythic patterns has been thoroughly explored by two generations of scholars.

Hemingway's plot structures attest to his sense of mythic perception through his depictions of the quest of the hero, his fascination with the rites and rituals of the bullfight, and his constant search for appropriate ceremonies to mark significant rites of passage, as well as his acknowledged belief in the theory of the collective unconscious.

Steinbeck was familiar with the works of Jung and friendly with Joseph Campbell, who lived next door to Ed Ricketts for a while. The Arthurian cycle influenced his works, most notably *Tortilla Flat*; Steinbeck was very disappointed when neither readers nor reviewers grasped this influence. His short novels often read like parables. Fontenrose is only one of a number of scholars who, given some distance from the timely political issues Steinbeck was addressing, have come to understand that "traditional myths and legends have much to do with the form and content of Steinbeck's fiction."[2]

It is appropriate then, since all three do operate within a strong mythic framework, that the image of woman in their fiction should also represent that frame of reference. The indestructible woman in her many manifestations as Earth Mother, Terrible Mother, Demeter/Persephone does just that. Their common mythic bent is one valid explanation of their parallel interpretation of the function of woman in human survival.

If Frazer's explosion on the literary landscape can be said to have had a dynamic effect, Freud's was an atomic blast. His findings strongly influenced these three writers and in fact most of the writing of the first two-thirds of this century. Freud's inability to understand the female psyche and his perpetuation of the repressions of the Victorian concept of women's role through the sacrosanct organ of psychotherapy continued the timeworn pattern of man as subject, woman as object. Freud's findings about sexuality and the role of the subconscious were certainly liberating to women as well as to men, and I do not want to engage here in the battle about whether or not Freud should be the whipping boy for contemporary woman's problems. What is true is that Freud's works were universally popularized and many of his complex findings or even unproven hypotheses were turned into popular mythology and were considered by many to be as irrefutable as explanations for human behavior and destiny as Genesis had been to earlier generations. This popularized Freudianism held that anatomy is destiny, and for women that meant a destiny circumscribed by their reproductive organs. Women who were not content with that limitation were told by their therapists that they were not normal. A happy woman, one who was well adjusted according to the precepts of Freudian psychology, was one who fulfilled her role as the bearer of children, adjunct, and helpmate and accepted her domination by the male. It is only with the perfection of contraceptive techniques that woman has been able to choose between motherhood and other alternatives. Undesired pregnancies are a recurrent source of conflict in the works of all three of these writers.

Another Freudian view that finds credence in the works of these three men is Freud's attitude toward the mother/son relationship. Freud attested to the universality of the Oedipal complex, and the recurrent mother figures, both fearsome and nurturant, in Faulkner, Hemingway, and Steinbeck are often reflections of their own preoccupations with the mother/son relationship.

Freud's reservations about women's roles in the development of civilization caused him to view them in a negative light. Faulkner, Hemingway, and Steinbeck, with their more primitivistic vision of women, shared a very different view of their value. In *Civilization and Its Discontents,* Freud explicitly indicts woman as enemy to man's higher development:

> Women soon come into opposition to civilization and display their retarding and restraining influence. . . . Women represent the interest of the family and of sexual life. The work of civilization has become increasingly the business of men, it confronts them with ever more difficult tasks and compels them to carry out instinctual sublimations of which women are little capable.[3]

Though civilization was a positive goal to a man of Freud's cosmopolitan sensibilities, Faulkner, Hemingway, and Steinbeck cast a jaundiced eye at the purported advances and "instinctual sublimations" of modern life. Therefore, insofar as woman, as seen by the Freudian thinker, was at odds with civilization, and insofar as these three writers distrusted civilization and its effects, it is quite fitting that women should have the positive function that they do in their works. The indestructible woman as an anticivilizational force works in a positive manner. Unimpressed by or uninvolved in the works of "progress," she keeps her eye on the primal issues, such as survival.

In the preceding chapters I have suggested some reasons why, because of individual personality and cultural milieu, each author should have created the kinds of women he did in his fiction. Faulkner's indestructible women are decidedly mythic. Three myths predominate: that of the bounteous Earth Mother, fecund and nature bound, such as Eula Varner or Lena Grove; that of Demeter/Persephone, the Eternal Feminine endlessly perpetuated through mother and daughter as in the cases of Addie and Dewey Dell, Caddy and Quentin II, and Eula and Linda; and the regional myth of the southern woman whose fragile looks belie her spine of steel, such as Granny Millard, Miss Habersham, or Miss Jenny DuPre. While the women in Faulkner's novels function in the roles of grandmothers, sisters, sweethearts, servants, children, mothers, aunts, spinsters, or wives, the women in Hemingway's novels are generally restricted to playing one of two roles, love object or sex object. In terms of their mythic roles, they are bitch-goddesses or corn goddesses, projections of the Terrible Mother or the Nurturing Mother. Earth mothers abound in Steinbeck; the other predominant myth that underlies his depiction of women is the myth of the whore with the heart of gold.

There is great variation in the detailing of the portraits of these indestructible women, but one inescapable particular that unites and interrelates their characterizations is that in both her most positive and most destructive versions woman is usually painted in maternal imagery. Be she a black matriarch and surrogate mother to white children such as Dilsey, a symbolic mother to the stranger, the ravished, and the group such as Pilar, or a woman who is so closely identified with her maternal role that she has no first name other than Ma (Joad), the most beneficent, the least ambiguously portrayed, and most heroic of the indestructible women in the novels of Faulkner and Steinbeck are the strong matriarchal figures. The deadly and devouring mothers are also present, some in their biological role as mother such as Mrs. Adams, others only as nominal mothers who treat their men like children such as Margot Macomber.

Given the personal histories of these authors, the ubiquity of maternal figures is not surprising. All of these men had mothers who were the dominant figures in their childhoods, the figures of strength and power in their formative years. Faulkner had not one but two venerable matriarchs to guide his development. Maud Butler Faulkner was assisted in the raising of the Faulkner boys by Caroline Barr, a woman who was in the words of Faulkner "the fount of authority over my conduct and of security for my physical welfare, and of active and constant affection and love."[4] Hemingway grew to hate his mother, which may partially explain why, though he portrays his women as behaving in "mothering" fashions in both destructive and nurturing modes, there are very few actual biological mothers in his works. George Mors, Steinbeck's roommate at Stanford, remembers that Olive Hamilton Steinbeck ruled the roost in the Steinbeck family. In his words, when she yelled frog, they all jumped.[5] She not only corrected her children's behavior, she also corrected her husband.

Each of these writers responded in a different manner to his upbringing in a woman-dominated household. Faulkner stayed close to home and visited his mother almost daily, remaining the devoted son though he also became, in effect, the patriarch of the family. Hemingway rarely visited his mother, barely suffered her visiting him, reviled her publicly, and did not even attend her funeral. Steinbeck, while he did not remain as close to his mother as Faulkner was to his, moved back into the family home to care for his mother during her final days, washing the sheets and helping with other household duties. During her lifetime, he was rarely financially independent of his parents.

And yet though each of these writers had a different relationship with his mother, there are close correspondences between their subsequent behaviors and the fact that powerful women were the dominant figures in their formative years. Both Hemingway and Steinbeck developed into men who throughout their lives continued to be dependent on women for their care and well-being. Hemingway's dependence was not only emotional but also financial. Grace Hemingway was often the primary financial provider in the Hemingway household. When she married Ed Hemingway she was earning close to $1000 a month while he earned only about $50.[6] Both the family home on Kenilworth Avenue and later her getaway cabin were built with her own funds. Thus financial dependence on women was not foreign to Ernest, who easily accepted being maintained by his first and second wives. In the greater part of his marriage to Hadley, the bulk of their subsistence was provided by Hadley's trust funds and legacies. These funds were not great, but sufficient. Ernest's pattern of financial dependency did not change with his second marriage; only the munificence of the support did. Pauline Peiffer was from a wealthy family and she and her Uncle Gus provided generously for Ernest, and even his son from the previous marriage, throughout the marriage. A number of biographers have suggested that Pauline's money was one of the reasons Hemingway was attracted to her. Meyers claims that "Hemingway felt his lack of money seriously limited his freedom and was attracted to her fortune."[7] Even after his writing brought him great financial success, his third wife, Martha Gellhorn, paid her own way in the marriage. Steinbeck, too, began his married life dependent on his first wife's earning capacity and his parents' generosity to provide minimum maintenance. He and Carol often lived in his parents' Pacific Grove vacation house; their finances were subsidized by a monthly allotment from his parents. When their funds were exhausted, Carol often worked at a job all day and then typed John's manuscripts at night.

Besides their willingness to be supported financially by women, both Hemingway and Steinbeck exhibited a decided emotional dependency on women. Hemingway married four times, but he never left one woman unless he had another ready to marry. In his marriages he was used to being spoiled and catered to. Hadley was willing to devote not only herself but all her resources to his will. She, who had been brought up in a reserved household, became a drinking companion and outdoorswoman. Though Hemingway always had enough funds for drink and travel, Hadley was often without appropriate clothes. Pauline, if possible, devoted even more of herself to Ernest. Unlike Hadley, who was often left behind to take care of their son Bumby, Pauline was wealthy enough to hire people to take care of the children she had with Hemingway. Thus her role as mother never superseded her role as wife. She was always available to him, ready to cater to his every whim.

Even before marriage, in his first important male/female relationship, Hemingway was in the position of being cared for by a woman. As his nurse, Agnes von Kurowsky pampered and catered to her young patient. Financial independence came relatively late in Hemingway's life. Prior to that time the women who cared for his needs, financial, physical, and emotional, were all older than he, mothers or mother figures. His emotional dependence on women continued to the end of his life—he always needed a woman waiting on him—but the women got progressively younger, daughter figures. Mary Hemingway, his last wife, was caretaker, whipping boy, and nurse, so submissive to Ernest's will that she became, in her own words, "an appendage."[8] His last great love, Adriana Ivancich, was young enough to be his granddaughter.

Steinbeck's best writing came out of those years when he could depend on Carol not only to help care for him and provide for his creature comforts, but also to provide a strong editorial hand for his works. Carol did more than transcribe John's longhand into type; as Steinbeck's son Thom explained, "Manuscripts would never have gotten to New York without her."[9] Carol strengthened weak sentences, provided punctuation, excised excessive sentimentality. She fed and fertilized his literary field, furnishing some of his best titles and introducing him to friends who provided interesting subject matter which he utilized in his writing.[10] In his marriages to Gwen and then Elaine, a failure on their parts to mother him would send him into deep depression.[11] After one such episode with Elaine, he began seeing Gertrudis Brenner, a counselor who helped him through a difficult period of self-doubt. The teachers who encouraged Steinbeck's writing were women; the agents who counseled him, represented him, and saw to his financial benefits were women. Steinbeck's dependence upon women touched many facets of his life.[12]

Though unhappily married, Faulkner remained with Estelle till his death. Theirs was not a relationship from which he drew either financial or emotional sustenance—in fact, the opposite. Estelle created financial problems for Faulkner, buying more than they could afford, mounting up debts. Her emotional problems were also a drain on his psychic energies. Faulkner's mother remained the model woman in his life. In a recent interview Jill Faulkner Summer explains, "I think that probably Pappy's idea of women—ladies—always revolved a great deal around Granny. She was just a very determined, tiny old lady that Pappy adored. Pappy admired so much in Granny and he didn't find it in my mother and I don't think he found it in anybody."[13] The figure of power and sustenance from his earliest days remained that figure throughout his life.

All human beings are dependent, some to greater degrees than others. The fact of a dominant matriarchal figure and a weak or passive patriarchal figure during the formative years is one possible explanation for the characterizations of indestructible women in Faulkner, Hemingway, and Steinbeck. Hemingway and Steinbeck's continued dependence on women throughout their lives and Faulkner's perpetual adoration of his mother are certainly significant features in a biographically oriented explanation. Women's strength and dependability were givens in the realities of their lives.

One other biographical factor may have relevance here. All three of these men had alcohol problems. Faulkner's alcoholism was the most acute. Modern diagnosis might conclude that his was an inherited disease, since it is known that his father and grandfather both drank excessively. When he drank, Faulkner often had horrible accidents. Once in New York he passed out in his hotel room, fell against a radiator, and quite literally cooked himself all night long. During one of his last drinking bouts he fell off his horse and hurt himself badly. Faulkner's alcoholism did destroy him; quite simply, he drank himself to death. Hemingway did not wait for drink to destroy him—he used a shotgun. However, during his lifetime his drinking did considerable damage. Hemingway was accident prone all his life and often the accidents were associated with heavy drinking. The irony is that Hemingway connected drinking and masculinity. Steinbeck's drinking eventually had to be stopped because of its negative effect on his health. He had a natural tendency toward depression, and alcohol, being a depressant, often sent him into severe states of melancholy. During all three of his marriages, drunken states often resulted in fights.

The alcoholic personality is both dependent and self-destructive. Menninger theorizes that the self-destructive drive in the alcoholic derives from guilt associated with the child's anger toward its parents. This anger results from the removal of oral gratification, most probably by the mother. The child cannot handle the guilt associated with the rage it feels against the parents and its consequent desire to destroy them which is accompanied by terror at losing them. In adulthood alcohol is then used as a means of both substitute oral gratification and revenge.[14] Knight characterizes the alcoholic personality as self-indulgently demanding of attention and affection.[15]

Biographical hypotheses are seductive, but what they have to tell us of the genesis of fictional creations provides only partial answers. Fiedler contends that literature comes into being when signature, the author's individual experience, is stamped on archetype. Certainly that definition is relevant here. The archetype of the Great Mother is stamped with each man's personal experience of women, both powerful and threatening, nurturing and withholding.

Another possible explanation for the profusion of earth mother figures in the works of these three men could be a result of the strong strain of nostalgia in their works. Each writes with special sensitivity about the pains of growing up. There is a marked disillusion with the world of their adulthood. Faulkner, in such works as *The Reivers, Intruder in the Dust*, and "The Bear," wistfully recreates youthful experiences when color did not divide playmates, when children capered together, unmindful of society's divisive strictures. In the early Nick Adams stories Hemingway recalls days of hunting and fishing in the North Woods, times of relative safety, before the trauma of war and wounds. Steinbeck revives both the carefree joys and the hard lessons of boyhood in *The Red Pony* and in selected episodes of *East of Eden*. The Ruthie and Winfield scenes in *The Grapes of Wrath* capture the sense of adventure of children in even the worst times for adults. None of these men had terrible childhoods. They were brought up with strong family support systems in a world open to the joys of the out-of-doors. Childhood was a time of innocence. In their works children, like Indians, Negroes, and peasants, are primitives, not yet burdened with the complexities of contemporary existence, innocent in nature, free to enjoy its bounties. Some of Faulkner, Hemingway, and Steinbeck's indestructible women are a re-creation of the bountiful and nurturing mother of that childhood. In simplistic terms she is the mother we all want when we are sick or hurt. Rare is the individual who doesn't long for the irresponsibility of childhood when mother was there to fix it all or make it better. In some ways, the indestructible woman for these men is like Prince Charming for women, a savior figure we hope will come along to keep us from having to face our problems.

This study began with the cataloguing of critical complaints against American male novelists in general and Faulkner, Hemingway, and Steinbeck, in particular, for their refusal to allow full humanity to women. Unable to see women as anything but *other*, they are supposed to be at such variance with the androgynous ideal that they perpetuate a restrictive cycle that commits men to violence and women to submission, thereby undermining individual human freedom. Generally, this criticism is apt. Yet each writer did, on occasion, transcend those limitations. Linda Snopes is a mature, intelligent, active, and sympathetic human being. Brett Ashley's unique morality and coping mechanisms are accounted for sympathetically. Pilar and Maria are strong and admirable survivors. Ma Joad's seeming imperturbability may appear too good to be true, but the toll it takes on her privately is also shown. True, richly detailed female characters such as these are few. But for Faulkner, Hemingway, and Steinbeck it is as often as not the dehumanized or sketchily drawn woman whose indestructibility is celebrated. The scarcity of fully drawn women in Hemingway and Steinbeck results from their male focus, their absorption with the male quest. The female is pathologically depicted in Faulkner, but so is the male; there are few positively characterized, fully human males in the obfuscated, miasmic world of Yoknapatawpha.

There is some obvious misogyny in these characterizations of women. Woman is often viewed through a glass darkly, deprived of her voice or not there at all. Still, when she is there, she can be the repository of the values, sometimes more than the man, absorbing all tragedy, enduring all the buffets of fortune, a stoic, indestructible figure. Joan Hedrick has called this conception of woman a "child's myth."[16] In her study of the problems in gender relationships that develop as a direct result of the maternal parent's having almost sole responsibility for infant care during the formative years, Dorothy Dinnerstein explains how such a myth would grow out of that relationship. Dinnerstein claims that the unconscious connection between woman and nature is formed in that period when the infant cannot distinguish between self and the outside world, when the mother is a "global, inchoate, all-embracing presence."[17] Thus the concepts of Mother Earth and Earth Mother are inextricably bound together. In either case the feminine is seen as the source of inexhaustible resources which, if they are not given to man voluntarily, can be forced from her. "Our over-personification of nature, then is inseparable from our under-personification of woman."[18] Such an accusation is not irrelevant to the characterization of women, particularly the enduring ones, in Faulkner, Hemingway, and Steinbeck.

For men with dependent and self-destructive personalities, longing for a simpler world, woman personifies what he is not, the *other*. The dependent man, then, would project a dependable other; the self-destructive man, an indestructible other. For men who all had terrible bouts with depression, is it not appropriate that the *other* should also serve as a symbol of optimism?

Notes

Chapter 1

1. "The American Woman," *Time*, 20 March 1972, p. 27.

2. Diane Gersoni Stavn, "Reducing the 'Miss Muffet' Syndrome: An Annotated Bibliography," *Library Journal*, 15 January 1972, p. 257.

3. Carolyn Heilbrun, "The Masculine Wilderness of the American Novel," *Saturday Review*, 29 January 1972, p. 41.

4. Ibid., p. 44.

5. Judith Fetterley, *The Resisting Reader* (Bloomington: Indiana University Press, 1978), p. xii.

6. Kate Millett, *Sexual Politics* (Garden City, N.Y.: Doubleday & Company, 1969).

7. Wendy Martin in "Seduced and Abandoned in the New World: The Fallen Woman in American Fiction," from her book *Woman in Sexist Society*, stresses the fact that our male novelists persist in perpetuating the tradition of the fallen woman (a tradition that a woman must forgo her sexuality in order to be redeemed). Mary Ellman in *Thinking about Women* decries not only feminine stereotyping, but also "phallic criticism." Hortense Calisher in a 1970 article for a special issue of *Mademoiselle* comments on how the writers in America are rigidly bound by an ethic which associates the true heterosexual with the male. She comments on the American breed of writer "who too early got hung up on Hemingway's jockstrap."

8. Leslie Fiedler, *Love and Death in the American Novel*, rev. ed. (New York: Stein & Day, 1966), p. 288.

9. Simone de Beauvoir, *The Second Sex*, ed. and trans. H.M. Parshley (New York: Knopf, 1953). De Beauvoir applies this argument to continental and British as well as American writers.

10. The rejection of the concept of *other* by modern women has brought with it renewed interest in the myth of Lilith as a more creative and self-liberating first female archetype. See Lilly Rivlin, "Lilith: The First Woman," *MS*, December, 1972, pp. 92–97, 114–15.

11. Ernest van den Haag's review of *Sexual Politics* for *National Review*, 22 September 1970, suggests that Millett's choice of writers is biased. He sees Miller and Mailer as sitting ducks for feminists.

12. Edmund Wilson, "Ernest Hemingway," *Atlantic Monthly*, July, 1939, p. 45.

13. Carlos Baker, "The Mountain and the Plain," *Hemingway: The Writer as Artist* (Princeton University Press, 1956), p. 113.

14. Fiedler, p. 316.

15. Ibid., p. 319.

16. Ibid., p. 415.

17. Maxwell Geismar, *Writers in Crisis* (New York: Hill & Wang, 1961), p. 168.

18. Ibid., pp. 179-80.

19. Gail Mortimer, *Faulkner's Rhetoric of Loss: A Study in Perception and Meaning* (Austin: University of Texas Press, 1983), p. 122.

20. Peter Lisca, *The Wide World of John Steinbeck* (Brunswick, N.J.: Rutgers University Press, 1958), p. 206.

21. Ibid., p. 207.

22. Robert Morsberger, "Steinbeck's Happy Hookers," *Steinbeck's Women: Essays in Criticism*, ed. Tetsumaro Hayashi, Steinbeck Monograph Series, No. 9, 1979, pp. 36-48.

23. Claude-Edmonde Magny, "Book Review of John Steinbeck's *East of Eden*," trans. Louise Varese, *Perspective USA*, 5, Fall, 1953, p. 147.

24. Walter E. Kidd, "Introduction," *American Winners of the Nobel Prize*, eds. Walter E. Kidd and Warren G. French (Norman: University of Oklahoma Press, 1968), p. 5.

25. Gustaf Hellstrom, "Presentation Address," *Nobel Prize Library* (New York: Alexis Gregory, 1971), p. 6.

26. The texts of these comments on Hemingway's tragic vision are included in Baker's "The Spanish Tragedy," Guttman's "Mechanized Doom," and Burhans's "*The Old Man and the Sea*: Hemingway's Tragic Vision of Man." All the above articles are anthologized in *Ernest Hemingway: Critiques of Four Major Novels*, ed. Carlos Baker (New York: Charles Scribner's Sons, 1956).

27. Philip Young, *Ernest Hemingway: A Reconsideration* (University Park: Pennsylvania State University Press, 1966), p. 245.

28. Ken Moritz, "Ernest Hemingway," *American Winners of the Nobel Prize*, eds. Warren G. French and Walter G. Kidd (Norman: University of Oklahoma Press, 1968), p. 159.

29. Kidd, p. 14.

30. Freeman Champney, "John Steinbeck, Californian," *Steinbeck: A Collection of Critical Essays*, ed. Robert Murray Davis (Englewood Cliffs, N.J.: Prentice-Hall, 1972), p. 32.

31. The significance of using nonsexist language is illustrated by Faulkner's use of the term "man" in his Nobel speech. I use the term in my summary of his remarks because he did. Of course he was using the term generically, but the irony is that, as this study will demonstrate, he often meant not man, but woman.

32. John Steinbeck, "Acceptance Speech," *Nobel Prize Library* (New York: Alexis Gregory, 1971), p. 206.

33. Cultural primitivism, as defined by Thrall and Hibbard in *A Handbook to Literature*, is a belief that nature (what exists undisturbed by man's artifice) is preferable and fundamentally better than any aspect of man's culture (any area of human activity where, by art or craft, man has modified or ordered nature). It is a belief that distrusts artifice, logic, social and political organizations, rules and conventions. Chronological primitivism sees man's present sad state as the product of what culture and society have done to him. Both kinds of primitivism are present in the works of Faulkner, Hemingway, and Steinbeck.

34. There is a strong strain of anti-intellectualism in these writers as well. Woman, traditionally considered less rational and more emotional than man, would fare well in their works for that reason also.

35. I have chosen to use the adjective "indestructible" to describe the attitude toward women reflected in a substantial number of the female characters in the works of Faulkner, Hemingway, and Steinbeck because of the connotations of that word in relation to the archetypal symbolism relating to women and matter. However, often terms such as enduring, strong, or indomitable will be used as alternatives. While these adjectives are not exactly synonymous, the character type that I am describing can be a composite of all or several of those qualities.

36. Floyd C. Watkins, *The Flesh and the Word* (Nashville: Vanderbilt University Press, 1971), p. 5. Watkins covers the movement from objectiveness to abstraction, from flesh to word of Eliot, Faulkner, and Hemingway. Steinbeck followed the same pattern, even noting to himself that in his early writing he had attempted to write like Hemingway, but by the time of *East of Eden* he had become more like Fielding. As Watkins explains, all the hard young men softened as they grew older.

37. Erich Neumann, *Amor and Psyche: The Psychic Development of the Feminine* (New York: Princeton University Press, 1956), p. 149.

38. Florida Scott-Maxwell, *Women and Sometimes Men* (London: Routledge & Kegan Paul, 1957), p. 192 (my emphasis).

39. Scott-Maxwell, p. 36.

Chapter 2

1. Frederick L. Gwynn and Joseph L. Blotner, eds., *Faulkner in the University* (Charlottesville: University of Virginia Press, 1959), p. 47.

2. Ibid., p. 72.

3. Ibid., p. 95.

4. Joseph Blotner, *William Faulkner's Library—A Catalogue* (Charlottesville: University of Virginia Press, 1964).

5. David Minter, *William Faulkner: His Life and Work* (Baltimore: Johns Hopkins University Press, 1980), pp. 72–73.

6. Ilse Dusoir Lind, "Faulkner's Women," *The Maker and The Myth: Faulkner and Yoknapatawpha 1977*, eds. Evans Harrington and Ann J. Abadie (Jackson: University Press of Mississippi, 1978), pp. 89–104. Lind presents a strong argument that Faulkner read both Dr. Louis Berman's *The Glands Regulating Personality* and Dr. Havelock Ellis's *Studies in the Psychology of Sex* and that those works influenced his characterizations of neurotic women.

7. Blotner, *Faulkner's Library*. Blotner catalogues the Faulkner libraries at Rowan Oak in Oxford as well as the volumes Faulkner chose to bring with him while he was writer-in-residence at the University of Virginia. Blotner notes which books had Faulkner's autograph, an indication that Faulkner loved that particular book. He also indicates which books looked as if they had never been opened.

8. Gwynn and Blotner, *Faulkner in the University*, p. 203.

9. Ibid., p. 251.

10. Richard P. Adams, *Faulkner: Myth and Motion* (Princeton: Princeton University Press, 1968), p. 10.

11. Thadious Davis, *Faulkner's "Negro": Art and the Southern Context* (Baton Rouge: Louisiana State University Press, 1983), pp. 6, 26.

12. Gwynn and Blotner, *Faulkner in the University*, p. 45.

13. Ibid., p. 74.

14. Ibid., p. 199.

15. Sally R. Page, *Faulkner's Women: Characterization and Meaning* (Deland, Fla.: Everett Edwards Inc., 1972), p. 52.

16. Gwynn and Blotner, *Faulkner in the University*, p. 1.

17. Eric J. Sundquist, *Faulkner: The House Divided* (Baltimore: Johns Hopkins University Press, 1983), pp. 3–27. Sundquist thinks there is good reason to question the centrality of this whole scene.

18. To avoid confusion between Caddy's daughter Quentin and her brother Quentin, I will refer to the daughter as Quentin II.

19. Erich Neumann, *The Great Mother*, trans. Ralph Manheim (Princeton: Princeton University Press, 1972), p. 47.

20. Wolfgang Lederer, M.D., *The Fear of Women* (New York: Harcourt Brace Jovanovich, 1968), p. 122.

21. Karl Jung, *The Psychology of the Unconscious*, trans. R.F.C. Hull (Princeton: Princeton University Press, 1953), p. 390.

22. M. Esther Harding, *Woman's Mysteries* (New York: Bantam Books, 1973), p. 21.

23. William Faulkner, *Essays, Speeches and Public Letters*, ed. James B. Merriweather (New York: Random House, 1965), p. 42.

24. Gwynn and Blotner, *Faulkner in the University*, p. 46.

25. Ibid., p. 249.

26. Ibid., p. 202. Faulkner mentions Ellen Glasgow as a writer he admired. The supposedly delicate but quite competent southern woman appears in her works. See especially *A Sheltered Life*. Scarlet O'Hara and Amanda Wingfield are variations on this theme.

27. Meta Carpenter Wilde and Orin Borsten, *A Loving Gentleman* (New York: Simon & Schuster, 1976). Meta Carpenter describes how on some occasions she had the feeling of being "treasured and pedestaled" (p. 79), while on other occasions Faulkner would expect her to be tough and stoic. When she broke down and cried about problems in her life, he rebuked her (p. 237).

28. Calvin C. Hernton, *Sex and Racism in America* (New York: Grove Press, Inc., 1965). Hernton's book argues the interconnectedness of sexual and racial myths and what he calls the sexualization of racism. See also Naomi Weisstein, "Stimulus/Response: Woman as Nigger," *Psychology Today*, Vol. 3, October, 1969, pp. 20–22, 58.

29. Davis, p. 3.

30. Nancy M. Tischler, *Black Masks: Negro Characters in Modern Southern Fiction* (University Park: Pennsylvania State University Press, 1969), pp. 32–33.

31. *Go Down Moses* (1942) was dedicated to Mammy Caroline Barr, Mississippi [1840–1940].

32. Hernton, p. 116.

33. Ibid., p. 97. See also Eric J. Sundquist's chapter on *Absalom, Absalom!* in *Faulkner: The House Divided* for a useful discussion of the issue of miscegenation.

34. Hernton, p. 51.

35. Gwynn and Blotner, *Faulkner in the University*, p. 31.

36. Carvel Collins, "The Pairing of *The Sound and the Fury* and *As I Lay Dying*," *Princeton University Library Chronicle*, 18 (Spring, 1957). pp. 119–20.

37. Adams, p. 59.

38. Walter Brylowski, *Faulkner's Olympian Laugh* (Detroit: Wayne State University Press, 1968), p. 12.

39. Sir James Frazer, *The Golden Bough*, one-volume abridged edition (New York: Macmillan Co., 1922), pp. 456–57. This is the edition Faulkner used.

40. C.G. Jung and C. Kerenyi, *Essays on a Science of Mythology*, trans. R.F.C. Hull (Princeton: Princeton University Press, 1959), p. 104.

41. Kerenyi, p. 107.

42. Ibid., p. 109.

43. Wilde and Borsten, p. 77. Meta Carpenter speaks of her dismay at Faulkner's need to turn her into a "girl-child," "to edit out all the facts of my life." Caddy, the "girl-child" of the book Faulkner considered one of his best, is referred to as his "heart's darling." Minter suggests that he saw the movement from girlhood to womanhood as almost the epitome of the Fall (Minter, 109). He bemoaned the maturation of his own daughter Jill (Blotner, *Faulkner*, p. 1169).

44. Kerenyi, p. 110.

45. Ibid., p. 109.

46. Ibid., p. 162.

47. Neumann, p. 309.

48. Gwynn and Blotner, *Faulkner in the University*, p. 251.

49. Robert Linscott, "Faulkner without Fanfare," *Esquire* 60 (July, 1963), p. 38.

50. Sally Page, Karl Zink, David Williams, Robert Kindrick are names that come immediately to mind. A comprehensive list might fill this page.

51. Irving Howe, *William Faulkner: A Critical Study* (New York: Random House, 1952), p. 131.

52. Fiedler, p. 320.

53. Richard Stonesifer, "In Defense of Dewey Dell," *Educational Leader*, 22 (July, 1958), p. 27.

54. David Williams, *Faulkner's Women: The Myth and the Muse* (Montreal: McGill-Queen's University Press, 1977), p. 225.

55. Faulkner, *Essays*, p. 42.

56. For a fuller discussion of Snopesism as the personification of the male principle see "The Male and Female Principles: The Snopes Trilogy," in Sally R. Page's *Faulkner's Women: Characterization and Meaning*.

57. Patricia Elizabeth Sweeney, *An Annotated Bibliography of Criticism of Women Characters in William Faulkner's Criticism*, DAI, 1983.

58. Cleanth Brooks, "Primitivism in *The Sound and the Fury*," *English Institute Essays 1952* (New York: Columbia University Press, 1954), p. 18.

59. David M. Miller, "Faulkner's Women," *Modern Fiction Studies*, 13 (Spring, 1967), p. 3.

60. Elizabeth M. Kerr, "William Faulkner and the Southern Concept of Woman," *Mississippi Quarterly*, 15 (Winter, 1961–62), p. 2.

61. Naomi Jackson, "Faulkner's Women: Demon-Nun and Angel-Witch," *Ball State University Forum*, 8 (Winter, 1967), p. 12.

62. Edith Hamilton, "Faulkner: Sorcerer or Slave?" *The Saturday Review*, 12 July 1952, p. 9.

63. Ibid., p. 9.

64. Ibid., p. 39.

65. Ibid., p. 40.

66. Maxwell Geismar, "A Rapt and Tumid Power," *The Saturday Review*, 12 July 1952, p. 10.

67. Walter Taylor, *Faulkner's Search for a South* (Urbana: University of Illinois Press, 1983). Taylor argues that despite Faulkner's conscious attempts to fight the prejudices of his upbringing, Faulkner never fully emancipated himself from the stereotyping of the society in which he was raised.

68. Melvin Backman, "Sickness and Primitivism: A Dominant Pattern in William Faulkner's Work," *Accent*, 14 (Winter, 1954), p. 62.

69. Ibid.

70. Ibid.

71. Brooks, "Primitivism," p. 6.

72. Ibid., p. 23.

73. Howe, p. 94.

74. Ibid., p. 99.

75. Edmond L. Volpe, *A Reader's Guide to William Faulkner* (New York: Farrar, Straus & Giroux, 1964), p. 27.

76. Ibid.

77. Olga W. Vickery, *The Novels of William Faulkner* (Baton Rouge: Louisiana State University Press, 1964), p. 289.

78. Ibid., p. 293.

79. Carvell Collins, "Nathanael West's *The Day of the Locust* and *Sanctuary*," *Faulkner Studies*, 2 (Summer, 1953), p. 23.

80. Nathanael West, *Miss Lonelyhearts & The Day of the Locust* (New York: New Directions, 1969), p. 173.

81. Carvell Collins, "A Note on *Sanctuary*," *Harvard Advocate*, 135 (November, 1951), p. 16.

82. Collins, "*Locust* and *Sanctuary*," p. 24.

83. Gwynn and Blotner, *Faulkner in the University*, p. 72.

84. Sally R. Page gives this archetype its fullest exploration in her book *Faulkner's Women: Characterization and Meaning.*

85. Gail Mortimer analyzes paradox in Faulkner's characterization of women in a forthcoming article in *Women's Studies*, "The Smooth, Suave Shape of Desire: Paradox in Faulknerian Imagery of Women." Philip Weinstein in "Meditations on the Other: Faulkner's Rendering of Women," presented at the twelfth annual Faulkner and Yoknapatawpha Conference, questions the often quoted statement by Faulkner that he thought women were marvelous and much more fun to write about than men. Weinstein points out the sexism of that statement. One would not use that language to describe men. In his discussion of the women in four of Faulkner's major works, Weinstein shows how Faulkner's women are deprived of their voices and isolated, viewed through the perception of men who do not understand them, any more than we the readers do.

86. Wilde and Borsten. Meta Carpenter speaks of being confounded by Faulkner's "need to turn her into a sweet, tremulous girl." The fantasy was so strong that Faulkner even bought her such inappropriate presents as ribbons for her hair.

87. Lederer, p. 249.

88. Kerenyi, p. 119.

89. Annette Kolodny, *The Lay of the Land* (Chapel Hill: University of North Carolina Press, 1975). Kolodny details the feminization of the land in the metaphors used by early explorers and settlers of this country. Though the concept of the land as woman is as ancient as history, in America it took on added significance according to Kolodny, for "the move to America was experienced as the daily reality of what has become the single dominating metaphor: regression from the cares of adult life and a return to the primal warmth of womb or breast in a feminine landscape" (p. 6).

90. Neumann, p. xlii.

Chapter 3

1. John Killinger explains in *Hemingway and the Dead Gods* (Lexington: University of Kentucky Press, 1960), "Love can never mean everything to the hero because to live authentically, he must remain *alone* in the presence of death" (p. 96).

2. Donald L. Kaufman, "The Long Happy Life of Norman Mailer," *Modern Fiction Studies* 17 (Autumn, 1971), pp. 347–59. Kaufman claims that Hemingway and Mailer are a "kind of

Siamese twins." Both of their worldviews stem from the "neo-primitve, a distrust of civilization and complication." In these worlds, Kaufman explains, "females end up as second class."

3. Budd Schulberg, *The Four Seasons of Success* (Garden City, N.Y.: Doubleday & Company), 1972, p. 130. Schulberg recounts a telephone conversation with Scott Fitzgerald, who according to Schulberg worshipped Hemingway, yet was able to see his faults. Fitzgerald did not think well of Hemingway's female characterizations: "Ernest knows how man fights wars, blows bridges, holds out, surrenders, dies—he's really in the big league when it comes to men dying—not so good on women dying—in fact when it comes to women in general, I don't think Ernest has learned a single thing about women since he was a junior in Oak Park High School."

4. Willard Thorp, *American Writing in the Twentieth Century* (Cambridge: Harvard University Press, 1960), p. 191. See also Linda Wagner, "'Proud and Friendly and Gently': Women in Hemingway's Early Fiction," *College Literature,* Vol. 7, No. 3, Fall, 1980. Wagner quotes from an unpublished letter from Scott Fitzgerald which makes substantially the same criticism. While she does not disagree with this criticism of his female characters after 1929 (except for Pilar, Maria, and Marie Morgan), Wagner contends that in his early stories Hemingway was "sympathetic and skillfull" in his portrayal of women.

5. Edmund Wilson, "Hemingway: Gauge of Morale," *The Wound and the Bow* (Oxford: Oxford University Press, 1947), reprinted in McCaffery, *Ernest Hemingway.*

6. Fiedler, p. 316.

7. Katherine M. Rogers, *The Troublesome Helpmate* (Seattle: University of Washington Press, 1966), p. 257.

8. John W. Presley, "'Hawks Never Share': Women and Tragedy in Hemingway," *Fitzgerald/Hemingway Annual* 1973, pp. 243–57.

9. Carol H. Smith, "Women and the Loss of Eden in Hemingway's Mythology," in *Ernest Hemingway: The Writer in Context,* ed. James Nagel (Madison: University of Wisconsin Press, 1984), pp. 129–44.

10. Geismar's and Fiedler's observations on the matter have already been cited. Katherine M. Rogers claims that Faulkner's fear is projected onto the desperate male characters he created.

11. Caddy Compson's Herbert is one example although he does not retain the title long. Jason then acts as surrogate father. Eula Varner's Flem is another, although Gavin Stevens assumes paternal responsibilities also. Horace Benbow is Little Belle's stepfather. Jewel is not Anse Bundren's son. Byron Burch will be surrogate father to Lena Grove's child. Faulkner was stepfather to Estelle's two children by Cornell Franklin. He was also surrogate father to his brother Dean's daughter, seeing her through her education and giving her away at her wedding at Rowan Oak.

12. Philip Wylie, *A Generation of Vipers* (New York, Rinehart & Company, 1942), pp. 184–204. In the chapter titled "Common Women" Wylie defines "momism" and what he sees as America's mother problem.

13. Wagner, p. 245. Hemingway's attitude toward mothers was so vituperative that he even accused them of driving their husbands to suicide. Wagner cites an unpublished article in which Hemingway claims that the mothers of his generation contributed to the suicide of the fathers.

14. To recount Baker's already quoted statement about Hemingway's heroines as "an aspect of the poetry of things . . . meant to show a symbolic or ritualistic function in the service of the artist and the service of man" (p. 113).

15. See Joseph Campbell's *The Hero with a Thousand Faces* or Otto Rank's *The Myth of the Birth of the Hero* for particulars of the hero cycle. Other sources include: W.H. Auden's "The Quest Hero," Northrop Frye's *Anatomy of Criticism*, Norma Goodrich's *Myths of the Hero*, Dorothy Norman's *The Hero: Myth/Symbol/Image*.

16. Phillip Young, *Hemingway: A Reconsideration* (University Park: Pennsylvania State University Press, 1966), p. 263. See also Frederick Hoffman, *The 20's* (New York: Macmillan Co., 1949). Much of what Young has to say about Hemingway's reactions to his wounding follows the line of thinking set forth in Hoffman's discussion of the "unreasonable wound."

17. Scott Donaldson, *By Force of Will* (New York: Viking Press, 1977) p. xi.

18. Neumann, p. 12.

19. The ambivalent character of the Mother Goddess is evident in the relationship between fertility rites and blood sacrifices. Kali, the Mother Goddess of India, is a good example of a goddess who in her gracious manifestation bestows existence and suckles her creations at her breasts while in her dark manifestation she demands daily blood sacrifices.

20. Donaldson, pp. 162–63. Donaldson claims that after his portrayal of Catherine in *A Farewell to Arms*, modeled in part on Agnes and in part on Hadley, Hemingway rarely again created a believable and sympathetic woman. Hadley and Agnes remained ideals in his mind. The last three wives did not fare as well in his writing.

21. Harry Levin, "Observations on the Style of Ernest Hemingway," *Hemingway: A Collection of Critical Essays*, ed. Robert P. Weeks (Englewood Cliffs, N.J.: Prentice-Hall, 1962) pp. 84–85.

22. Bernice Kert, *The Hemingway Women* (New York: W.W. Norton & Company, 1983), p. 35.

23. Ibid., pp. 72–73.

24. Unpublished letter, Humanities Research Center, The University of Texas at Austin.

25. "Copy of letter handed to EMH, July 27, 1920," Unpublished letter, Humanities Research Center, The University of Texas at Austin.

26. Leicester Hemingway, *My Brother, Ernest Hemingway* (Greenwich, Conn.: Fawcett Publications, Inc., 1963), p. 60.

27. Ibid.

28. Ibid., p. 91.

29. Carlos Baker, *Ernest Hemingway: A Life Story* (New York: Charles Scribner's Sons, 1969), p. 465.

30. Max Westbrook, "Grace under Pressure: Hemingway and the Summer of 1920," in *Ernest Hemingway: The Writer in Context*, ed. James Nagel (Madison: University of Wisconsin Press, 1984), pp. 77–106.

31. Kert, pp. 63–64.

32. Baker, *A Life Story*, p. 50.

33. L. Hemingway, pp. 44–45.

34. Baker, *A Life Story*, p. 59.

35. Donaldson's reading of *A Farewell to Arms*, "Frederic Henry, Selfish Lover," asserts that not only does Catherine die, but "throughout their affair, Frederic rarely displays honest and thoughtful concern for Catherine's feelings" (p. 160).

36. Baker, *A Life Story*, p. 104.

37. Ibid., p. 178.

38. Ibid.

39. Donaldson's chapter "Not Getting over Hadley," pp. 148–51, summarizes Hemingway's various expressions of guilt in letters and remarks to friends.

40. George Plimpton, "The Art of Fiction XXI," *Paris Review* (Spring, 1958), p. 69.

41. Roger Whitlow, *Cassandra's Daughters* (Westport: Greenwood Press, 1984), p. 47.

42. Hemingway's interest in sexual relativity is expressed in a novel he never published titled *Garden of Eden*. In it, the hero and heroine experiment with sex role reversal. See Aaron Latham, "Unfinished Manuscripts Reveal a Hemingway No One Knew," *Chicago Tribune,* October 17, 1977, Sec. 3, p. 20. A number of his most appealing heroines either have mannish haircuts (Brett and Maria) or want to cut their hair to look like their lovers (Catherine). Pictures of Duff Twysdan, Hadley, and Pauline Peiffer show them all sporting mannish bobs.

43. Linda Wagner in her article about Hemingway's early heroines, "Proud and Friendly and Gently...," reprints portions of the original first two chapters of *The Sun Also Rises*, portions deleted before publication. Wagner explains that Hemingway intended Brett to be seen as a bereaved and betrayed war victim who carries it all off with style and grace.

44. Baker, p. 180.

45. Margot is not without her defenders. See Anne Greco, "Margot Macomber: Bitch Goddess, Exonerated," *Fitzgerald/Hemingway Annual* 1972, pp. 273–79. Also Warren Beck, "The Shorter Happy Life of Mrs. Macomber," *Modern Fiction Studies*, 21 (Autumn, 1975), pp. 363–76. Roger Whitlow calls her "the most critically maligned female character since Lady Macbeth," *Cassandra's Daughters*, p.59.

46. Bernard Oldsey, "Hemingway's Beginnings and Endings," *Ernest Hemingway: The Papers of a Writer* (New York: Garland Publishing, Inc., 1981) pp. 37–62. Oldsey quotes the unpublished typescript from Hemingway's "The Art of the Short Story" in which Hemingway calls Margot both "a bitch for the full course" and "no good to anybody now except for trouble." Obviously, Hemingway had in mind a destructive woman when he created her. While I sympathize with those critics who point out both Wilson's and Francis's lack of integrity and misconceptions about masculinity, it is obvious that they are bringing their own frame of reference to the story and ignoring the author's.

47. Oldsey, p. 50.

48. Oldsey, p. 54.

49. Baker, p. 341.

50. A number of critics do not share my positive reading of Pilar's character. Presley claims that "Hemingway clearly intends that Pilar be another castrating mother figure" (p. 7). In Presley's opinion Hemingway succeeded. He finds her essentially passive, never dominant,

and yet "the most castrating, the most masculine of Hemingway's female characters" (p. 8). It is hard to imagine that Hemingway would give a character whom he meant to portray negatively the same name as his boat, which he loved.

51. Chaman Nahal, *The Narrative Pattern in Ernest Hemingway's Fiction* (Rutherford: Fairleigh Dickinson University Press, 1971). In Nahal's opinion Pilar is "perhaps the finest female character drawn by Hemingway, perfect within the dimensions he allows her" (p. 137).

52. Samuel Shaw, *Ernest Hemingway* (New York: Frederick Ungar Publishing Co., 1973), p. 100.

53. John Atkins, *The Art of Ernest Hemingway: His Work and Personality* (London: Spring Books, 1964).

54. Whitlow mentions Pilar only three times, pp. 13, 34, 38, but never discusses her character. This omission is remarkable in a book subtitled "The Women in Hemingway."

55. Allen Guttmann, "'Mechanized Doom': Ernest Hemingway and the American View of the Spanish Civil War." *Ernest Hemingway: Critiques of Four Major Novels*, ed. Carlos Baker (New York: Charles Scribner's Sons, 1962). Guttmann dismisses her as "a kind of Iberian Earth Mother" (p. 98). Michael J. B. Allen, "The Unspanish War in *For Whom the Bell Tolls*," *Contemporary Literature*, 13, No. 2 (Spring, 1972), criticizes Maria's characterization, but not Pilar's (p. 212). Earl Rovit, *Ernest Hemingway* (New York: Twayne Publishing Co., 1963), complains that "Maria is somewhat too slight to hold the burden of symbolic meaning which is placed on her," ignoring Pilar's symbolic function (p. 146). Robert Brainard Pearsall, *The Life and Writing of Ernest Hemingway* (Amsterdam: Rodopi NV, 1973). The only time Pearsall mentions Pilar is to describe her as a "fat, ex-prostitute."

56. Arthur Waldhorn, *A Reader's Guide to Ernest Hemingway* (New York: Octagon Books, 1972), pp. 71–72.

57. Leonard Lutwack, *Heroic Fiction: The Epic Tradition and American Novels of the Twentieth Century* (Carbondale and Edwardsville: Southern Illinois University Press, 1971). Lutwack calls Pilar Maria's "protective goddess" (p. 73). Lutwack also makes the trenchant observation that Pilar, Ma Joad, and Dilsey share characteristics such as being larger-than-life survivors (p. 77).

58. Mark Schorer, "The Background of a Style," *Ernest Hemingway: Critiques of Four Major Novels*, ed. Carlos Baker (New York: Charles Scribner's Sons, 1962), p. 89.

59. Kert, p. 342.

60. Ibid., p. 299.

61. Maxwell Geismar, "To Have and To Have and To Have," *Saturday Review of Literature*, 23 (September 9, 1950), p. 18.

62. Norman Cousins, "Hemingway and Steinbeck," *Saturday Review of Literature* (October 28, 1950), p. 24.

63. Kert, p. 456.

64. Rovit, p. 65.

65. Young, p. 199.

66. Tom Burnam, "Primitivism and Masculinity in the Work of Hemingway," *Modern Fiction Studies* 1 (August, 1955), pp. 20–21.

67. Sister Mary Damascene Brocki, CSSF, "Faulkner and Hemingway: Values in a Modern World," *Mark Twain Journal* (Summer, 1962), p. 6.

Chapter 4

1. John Ditsky, "Faulkner Land and Steinbeck Country," *Steinbeck: The Man and His Work*, ed. Richard Astro and Tetsumaro Hayashi (Corvallis, Oreg.: Oregon State University Press, 1971), p. 11.

2. Ibid., p. 23.

3. Lester Jay Marks, *Thematic Design in the Novels of John Steinbeck* (The Hague: Mouton, 1971), p. 15.

4. Joan Hedrick, "Mother Earth and Earth Mother: The Recasting of Myth in *The Grapes of Wrath*," *The Grapes of Wrath: A Collection of Critical Essays* (Englewood Cliffs, N.J.: Prentice-Hall, 1982), p. 136. Hedrick's contention is that though the just quoted description is acceptable as a childlike view of the mother who seems all-competent, it is "not a realistic portrait of a woman." In Hedrick's view, Ma Joad never breaks or shows less than these suprahuman qualities.

5. Howard Levant, *The Novels of John Steinbeck: A Critical Study* (Columbia, Mo.: University of Missouri Press, 1974), p. 124.

6. Letter from Pascal Covici, January 9, 1939, quoted in *Steinbeck: A Life in Letters*, eds. Elaine Steinbeck and Robert Wallsten (New York: Viking Press, 1975), p. 177.

7. Letter to Pascal Covici, January 16, 1939, *Steinbeck: A Life in Letters*, p. 178.

8. Jackson J. Benson, *The True Adventures of John Steinbeck, Writer* (New York: The Viking Press, 1984), p. 395.

9. Martin Shockley, "Christian Symbolism in *The Grapes of Wrath*," reprinted in *A Casebook on The Grapes of Wrath*, ed. Agnes McNeil Donohue (New York: Thomas Y. Crowell Co., 1968), p. 94.

10. Eric W. Carlson, "Symbolism in *The Grapes of Wrath*," reprinted in *A Casebook on The Grapes of Wrath*, p. 100.

11. Frederic S. Carpenter, H. Kelly Crockett, Celest Turner Wright, Peter Lisca, Theodore Pollock, and Jules Chametzky are a few of the critics who have commented on the significance of the closing scene. Their remarks are anthologized in Donohue, *A Casebook on The Grapes of Wrath*.

12. Levant, p. 124.

13. Leonard Lutwack, *Heroic Fiction: The Epic Tradition and American Novels of the Twentieth Century* (Carbondale and Edwardsville: Southern Illinois University Press, 1971), p. 55.

14. See my article on "Ma Joad and Pilar: Significantly Similar," *Steinbeck Quarterly*, Vol. 14, Nos. 3 & 4 (Summer/Fall, 1981), pp. 93–104.

15. Marks, p. 106.

16. Warren French, *John Steinbeck* (New York, 1961), p. 138.

17. Harry Morris, "*The Pearl*: Realism and Allegory," *Steinbeck: A Collection of Critical Essays*, ed. Robert Murray Davis (Englewood Cliffs, N.J.: Prentice-Hall, 1972), p. 161.

18. Sandra Beatty, "A Study of Female Characterization in Steinbeck's Fiction," *Steinbeck's Women: Essays in Criticism*, ed. Tetsumaro Hayashi, Steinbeck Monograph Series, No. 9, 1979, p. 3.

19. In the Grimms' fairy tale "The Fisherman and His Wife," though the fisherman is able to secure consecutively greater luxuries, his wife is never content. Her constant nagging and greed cause them to lose everything he has gained.

20. "From Lady Brett to Ma Joad: A Singular Scarcity," presented at the Second International Steinbeck Congress, Salinas, August 2, 1984. To be published in the forthcoming Congress Proceedings.

21. Richard Astro, "Steinbeck's *Sea of Cortez*," *A Study Guide to Steinbeck: A Handbook of His Major Works*, ed. Tetsumaro Hayashi (Metuchen, N.J.: The Scarecrow Press, 1974), pp. 173–75.

22. Paul McCarthy, *John Steinbeck* (New York: Frederick Ungar Publishing Co., 1980). McCarthy's is a discerning discussion of Steinbeck's intertwining of the techniques of fiction with factual narrative in *Sea of Cortez*. See pp. 87–94.

23. Lisca, p. 290, and French, p. 161.

24. Benson, p. 413.

25. Gene Detro, "Carol—The Woman behind the Man," *The Sunday Peninsula Herald Weekend Magazine*, June 10, 1984, pp. 3–6. Detro has been authorized by Bill Brown, Carol's second husband, to write her biography. Detro quotes Thom Steinbeck, in a recent interview, as saying, "Manuscripts would never have gotten to New York without her [Carol]." In a second article, "The Truth about Steinbeck (Carol & John)," *Creative States Quarterly*, No. 2, Detro quotes Ed Ricketts, Jr.'s rememberance that his father considered Carol to be "the backbone of John's writing."

26. Edmund C. Richards, "Challenge of John Steinbeck," *North American Review* (Summer, 1937), p. 407.

27. Robert E. Morsberger, "Steinbeck's Happy Hookers," *Steinbeck's Women: Essays in Criticism*, ed. Tetsumaro Hayashi, pp. 36–48. Morsberger's assessment is that Steinbeck "treats the oldest profession with amused tolerance if not downright sentimentality" (p. 41).

28. Annette Kolodny, *The Lay of the Land: Metaphor as Experience and History in American Life and Letters* (Chapel Hill: University of North Carolina Press, 1975). Kolodny evidences the land-as-woman metaphor in the documents of explorers, colonists, and writers.

29. Peter Lisca, "Steinbeck's Image of Man," *Modern Fictional Studies*, 11 (Spring, 1968), p. 8.

30. Elaine Steinbeck and Robert Wallstein, eds., *Steinbeck: A Life in Letters* (New York: Viking Press, 1975), p. 304.

31. John Steinbeck, *Journal of a Novel: The East of Eden Letters* (New York: Viking Press, 1969), p. 195.

32. John Ditsky, *Essays on East of Eden*, Steinbeck Monograph Series, No. 7, 1977, p. 38. Ditsky explains that in this passage Steinbeck deliberately rejects an image he has often used before, that of caves or cavelike places in nature as places for retreat and refreshment. Abra will not let Caleb hide or symbolically return to the womb; she makes him face up to what he has done.

Chapter 5

1. In "From Lady Brett to Ma Joad: A Singular Scarcity," forthcoming in the proceedings of the Second International Steinbeck Congress, I have provided details about Steinbeck's many associations with professional women. The professors who most influenced him during his years at Stanford were Edith Ronald Mirrielees and Margery Bailey. His agents were Elizabeth Otis, Mavis MacIntosh and Annie Laurie Williams. He was introduced to labor organizers by Ella Winter, in whose home he learned about the work of Caroline Decker.

2. Joseph Fontenrose, *John Steinbeck: An Introduction and Interpretation* (New York: Barnes & Noble, 1963), p. v.

3. Sigmund Freud, *The Standard Edition of the Complete Psychological Works*, ed. and trans. James Strachey (London: Hogarth Press, 1964), 21, 103–4.

4. "Funeral Sermon for Mammy Caroline Barr," *Essays, Speeches, and Public Letters* (New York: Random House, 1965), p. 117.

5. "Panel: An Evening with Steinbeck Friends," *Steinbeck Festival V and the Second International Steinbeck Congress*, Salinas, Calif., August 4, 1984.

6. Jeffrey Meyer, *Hemingway: A Biography* (New York: Harper & Row, 1985), p. 6.

7. Ibid., p. 174.

8. Mary Welsh Hemingway, *How It Was* (New York: Alfred A. Knopf, 1976), p. 162. Both A.E. Hotchner in the new edition of *Papa Hemingway* and Bernice Kert in *Hemingway's Women* detail the humiliation and abuse Mary Hemingway took from Ernest.

9. Quoted in "The Truth about Steinbeck (Carol & John)," *Creative States Quarterly*, No. 2, (Carmel, Calif.), pp. 12–13, 16.

10. Carol's friend Sue Gregory handed over the transcriptions she had made of stories about the people who lived in what Steinbeck called "Tortilla Flat." Elizabeth Ingels, Carol's partner in an ill-fated advertising agency, during her visits with the Steinbecks told the stories that formed the foundation of *Pastures of Heaven*.

11. Jackson J. Benson, *The True Adventures of John Steinbeck, Writer* (New York: Viking Press, 1984), p. 744.

12. See note 1.

13. Spoken in a television interview, quoted in Joseph Blotner's one-volume edition of *Faulkner: A Biography*, p. 215.

14. Morris E. Chafetz, M.D., "Alcoholism and Alcoholic Psychosis," *Comprehensive Textbook of Psychiatry II*, eds. Alfred M. Freedman, M.D., Harold I. Kaplan, M.D., Benjamin J. Sadock, M.D. (Baltimore: The Williams & Wilkins Company, 1975), p. 1339.

15. Ibid.

16. Joan Hedrick, "Mother Earth and Earth Mother: The Recasting of Myth in Steinbeck's *The Grapes of Wrath*," *The Grapes of Wrath: A Collection of Critical Essays* (Englewood Cliffs, N.J.: Prentice-Hall, 1982), p. 143.

17. Dorothy Dinnerstein, *The Mermaid and The Minotaur* (New York: Harper Colophon Books, 1977), p. 93.

18. Ibid., p. 108.

Bibliography

Primary Sources

Faulkner, William. *Absalom, Absalom!* New York: Random House, 1936.
_____. *As I Lay Dying.* New York: Random House, 1930.
_____. *Essays, Speeches and Public Letters*, ed. James B. Merriweather. New York: Random House, 1965.
_____. *The Hamlet.* New York: Random House, 1940.
_____. *Intruder in the Dust.* Second Printing. Random House, 1948.
_____. *Light in August.* The Modern Library. New York: Random House, 1932.
_____. *The Mansion.* New York: Random House, 1959.
_____. *Sanctuary.* The Modern Library. New York: Random House, 1931.
_____. *Sartoris.* New York: Random House, 1956.
_____. *The Sound and the Fury and As I Lay Dying.* With Appendix. New York: Random House, 1946.
_____. *The Town.* New York: Random House, 1957.
_____. *The Unvanquished.* New York: Random House, 1965.
Hemingway, Ernest. *Across the River and into the Trees.* New York: Charles Scribner's Sons, 1950.
_____. *For Whom the Bell Tolls.* London: Jonathan Cape, 1963.
_____. *A Moveable Feast.* New York: Charles Scribner's Sons, 1964.
_____. *The Old Man and the Sea.* New York: Charles Scribner's Sons, 1960.
_____. *The Short Stories of Ernest Hemingway.* New York: Charles Scribner's Sons, 1960.
_____. *The Sun Also Rises.* New York: Charles Scribner's Sons, 1954.
_____. *To Have and Have Not.* New York: Charles Scribner's Sons, 1937.
Steinbeck, John. *Burning Bright.* New York: Viking Press, 1950.
_____. *East of Eden.* New York: Viking Press, 1952.
_____. *The Grapes of Wrath.* New York: Viking Press, 1939.
_____. *The Long Valley.* New York: Viking Press, 1938.
_____. *The Pastures of Heaven.* New York: Bantam Books, 1956.
_____. *The Pearl.* New York: Viking Press, 1947.
_____. *Sweet Thursday.* New York: Viking Press, 1954.
_____. *To a God Unknown.* New York: Bantam Books, 1960.

Secondary Sources: Books

Adams, Richard P. *Faulkner: Myth and Motion*. Princeton, N.J.: Princeton University Press, 1968.

Baker, Carlos. *Ernest Hemingway: A Life Story*. New York: Charles Scribner's Sons, 1969.

Benson, Jackson J. *The True Adventures of John Steinbeck, Writer*. New York: Viking Press, 1984.

Bleikasten, Andre. *Faulkner's As I Lay Dying*. Revised and Enlarged Edition. Trans. Roger Little. Bloomington: Indiana University Press, 1973.

Blotner, Joseph. *Faulkner: A Biography*. One-Volume Edition. New York: Random House, 1984.

_____. *William Faulkner's Library—A Catalogue*. Charlottesville: University Press of Virginia, 1964.

Brylowski, Walter. *Faulkner's Olympian Laugh*. Detroit: Wayne State University Press, 1968.

Campbell, Joseph. *The Hero with a Thousand Faces*. Cleveland: World Publishing Co., 1956.

Cowley, Malcolm. *The Faulkner-Cowley File: Letters and Memories, 1944–1962*. New York: Viking Press, 1976.

Davis, Thadious. *Faulkner's "Negro": Art and the Southern Context*. Baton Rouge: Louisiana State University Press, 1983.

de Beauvoir, Simone. *The Second Sex*. New York: Bantam Books, 1961.

Dinnerstein, Dorothy. *The Mermaid and the Minotaur*. New York: Harper Colophon Books, 1977.

Donaldson, Scott. *By Force of Will*. New York: Viking Press, 1977.

Ellman, Mary. *Thinking about Women*. New York: Harcourt Brace Jovanovich, Inc., 1968.

Fetterley, Judith. *The Resisting Reader: A Feminist Approach to American Fiction*. Bloomington: Indiana University Press, 1978.

Fiedler, Leslie A. *Love and Death in the American Novel*. Revised Edition. New York: Stein and Day, 1966.

Fontenrose, Joseph. *John Steinbeck: An Introduction and Interpretation*. New York: Barnes & Noble, Inc., 1963.

Frazer, Sir James. *The Golden Bough*. One-Volume Abridged Edition. New York: Macmillan Co., 1922.

French, Warren G. *John Steinbeck*. New York: Twayne Publishers, Inc., 1961.

French, Warren G. and Walter E. Kidd, eds. *American Winners of the Nobel Literary Prize*. Norman: University of Oklahoma Press, 1968.

Freud, Sigmund. *The Standard Edition of the Complete Psychological Works*. Vol. 21. Ed. and Trans., James Strachey. London: The Hogarth Press, 1964.

Geismar, Maxwell. *Writers in Crisis*. New York: Hill and Wang, 1961.

Guerard, Albert J. *The Triumph of the Novel: Dickens, Dostoevsky, Faulkner*. New York: Oxford University Press, 1976.

Gwynn, Frederick L. and Joseph L. Blotner, eds. *Faulkner in the University*. Charlottesville: University Press of Virginia, 1959.

Harding, M. Esther. *Woman's Mysteries*. New York: Bantam Books, 1973.

Hemingway, Leicester. *My Brother: Ernest Hemingway*. Greenwich, Conn.: Fawcett Publications, Inc., 1963.

Hemingway, Mary. *How It Was*. New York: Alfred A. Knopf, 1976.

Hernton, Calvin C. *Sex and Racism in America*. Garden City, N.Y.: Doubleday & Co., Inc., 1965.

Hoffman, Frederick. *The 20's*. New York: Macmillan Co., 1949.

Hotchner, A. E. *Papa Hemingway: The Ecstasy and Sorrow*. New Edition. New York: Quill, 1983.

Howe, Irving. *William Faulkner: A Critical Study.* New York: Random House, 1952.

Jenkins, Lee. *Faulkner and Black-White Relations.* New York: Columbia University Press, 1981.

Jung, Carl. *The Psychology of the Unconscious.* Trans. R.F.C. Hull. Princeton, N.J.: Princeton University Press, 1953.

――――. and C. Kerenyi. *Essays on a Science of Mythology.* Trans. R.F.C. Hull. Bollinger Series 22. Princeton, N.J.: Princeton University Press, 1959.

Kert, Bernice. *The Hemingway Women.* New York: W.W. Norton & Company, 1983.

Kiernan, Thomas. *The Intricate Music: A Biography of John Steinbeck.* Boston: Little, Brown and Company, 1979.

Killinger, John. *Hemingway and the Dead Gods.* Lexington: University of Kentucky Press, 1960.

Koloc, Frederick Joseph. *John Steinbeck's In Dubious Battle: Backgrounds, Reputation and Artistry.* University of Pittsburgh, 1974. Unpublished dissertation.

Kolodny, Annette. *The Lay of the Land.* Chapel Hill: University of North Carolina Press, 1975.

Lederer, Wolfgang, M.D. *The Fear of Women.* New York: Harcourt Brace Jovanovich, 1968.

Levant, Howard. *The Novels of John Steinbeck.* Columbia, Mo.: University of Missouri Press, 1974.

Lisca, Peter. *The Wide World of John Steinbeck.* Brunswick, N.J.: Rutgers University Press, 1958.

Lutwack, Leonard. *Heroic Fiction: The Epic Tradition and American Novels of the Twentieth Century.* Carbondale and Edwardsville: Southern Illinois University Press, 1971.

Marks, Lester Jay. *Thematic Design in the Novels of John Steinbeck.* The Hague: Mouton, 1971.

McCaffery, John K.M., ed. *Ernest Hemingway: The Man and His Work.* Cleveland and New York: World Publishing Co., 1950.

McCarthy, Paul. *John Steinbeck.* New York: Frederick Ungar Publishing Co., 1980.

Meyers, Jeffrey. *Hemingway: A Biography.* New York: Harper & Row, 1985.

Millett, Kate. *Sexual Politics.* Garden City, N.Y.: Doubleday & Co., Inc., 1970.

Minter, David. *William Faulkner: His Life and Work.* Baltimore: Johns Hopkins University Press, 1980.

Mortimer, Gail L. *Faulkner's Rhetoric of Loss.* Austin: University of Texas Press, 1983.

Neumann, Erich. *Amor and Psyche.* Bollinger Series 54. New York: Pantheon Books, 1956.

――――. *The Great Mother.* Trans. Ralph Manheim. Bollinger Series. Princeton, N.J.: Princeton University Press, 1972.

Nobel Prize Library: Faulkner, O'Neill, Steinbeck. New York: Alexis Gregory, 1971.

Page, Sally R. *Faulkner's Women: Characterization and Meaning.* Deland, Fla.: Everett Edwards Inc., 1972.

Patterson, Angela. *The Women of John Steinbeck's Novels in the Light of Humanist Psychology.* United States International University, 1974. Unpublished dissertation.

Pitavy, François. *Faulkner's Light in August.* Revised and Enlarged Edition. Trans. Gillian E. Cook. Bloomington: Indiana University Press, 1973.

Rank, Otto. *The Myth of the Birth of the Hero.* New York: Alfred A. Knopf, Inc., 1959.

Rogers, Katherine M. *The Troublesome Helpmate.* Seattle: University of Washington Press, 1966.

Rovit, Earl. *Ernest Hemingway.* New York: Twayne Publishing Co., 1963.

Schulberg, Budd. *The Four Seasons of Success.* Garden City, N.Y.: Doubleday & Company, Inc., 1972.

Scott-Maxwell, Florida. *Women and Sometimes Men.* London: Routledge & Kegan Paul, 1957.

Sokoloff, Alice Hunt. *Hadley: The First Mrs. Hemingway.* New York: Dodd, Mead, & Company, 1973.

St. Pierre, Brian. *John Steinbeck: The California Years.* San Francisco: Chronicle Books, 1983.

Steinbeck, Elaine and Robert Wallsten, eds. *Steinbeck: A Life in Letters.* New York: Viking Press, 1975.

Steinbeck, John. *Journal of a Novel: The East of Eden Letters.* New York: Viking Press, 1969.

Sundquist, Eric J. *Faulkner: The House Divided.* Baltimore: Johns Hopkins University Press, 1983.

Sweeney, Patricia Elizabeth. *An Annotated Bibliography of Criticism of Women Characters in William Faulkner's Criticism.* DAI, 1983.

Taylor, Walter. *Faulkner's Search for the South.* Urbana: University of Illinois Press, 1983.

Thorp, Willard. *American Writers of the Twentieth Century.* Cambridge: Harvard University Press, 1960.

Thrall, William Flint and Addison Hibbard. *A Handbook to Literature.* Revised and Enlarged by C. Hugh Holman. New York: Odyssey Press, 1960.

Tischler, Nancy M. *Black Masks: Negro Characters in Modern Southern Fiction.* University Park: Pennsylvania State University Press, 1969.

Trilling, Lionel. *The Liberal Imagination.* Garden City, N.Y.: Anchor Books, 1953.

Valjean, Nelson. *John Steinbeck: The Errant Knight.* San Francisco: Chronicle Books, 1975.

Vickery, Olga W. *The Novels of William Faulkner.* Revised Edition. Baton Rouge: Louisiana State University Press, 1964.

Volpe, Edmond L. *A Reader's Guide to William Faulkner.* New York: Farrar, Straus, & Giroux, 1964.

Wagner, Linda Welshimer. *Ernest Hemingway: A Reference Guide.* Boston: G.K. Hall & Co., 1977.

————. *Hemingway and Faulkner: inventors/masters.* Metuchen, N.J.: Scarecrow Press, Inc., 1975.

Watkins, Floyd C. *The Flesh and the Word.* Nashville: Vanderbilt University Press, 1971.

West, Nathanael. *Miss Lonelyhearts & The Day of the Locust.* New York: New Directions, 1969.

Whitlow, Roger. *Cassandra's Daughters: The Women in Hemingway.* Westport, Conn.: Greenwood Press, 1984.

Williams, David. *Faulkner's Women: The Myth and the Muse.* Montreal: McGill-Queen's University Press, 1977.

Wittenberg, Judith Bryant. *Faulkner: The Transfiguration of Biography.* Lincoln: University of Nebraska Press, 1979.

Wilde, Meta Carpenter and Orin Borsten. *A Loving Gentleman.* New York: Simon & Schuster, 1976.

Young, Philip. *Ernest Hemingway: A Reconsideration.* University Park: Pennsylvania State University Press, 1966.

Secondary Sources: Articles

Allen, Mary. "Hail to Arms: A View of *For Whom the Bell Tolls.*" *Fitzgerald/Hemingway Annual 1973*, pp. 285–93.

"The American Woman." *Time,* 20 March 1972, pp. 25–104.

Astro, Richard. "Steinbeck's Sea of Cortez." *A Study Guide to Steinbeck: A Handbook of His Major Works.* Ed. Tetsumaro Hayashi. Metuchen, N.J.: The Scarecrow Press, Inc., 1974, pp. 173–75.

Backman, Melvin. "Sickness and Primitivism: A Dominant Pattern in William Faulkner's Work." *Accent,* 14 (Winter, 1954), 61–73.

Baker, Carlos. "The Mountain and the Plain." *Hemingway: The Writer as Artist.* Ed. Carlos Baker. Princeton, N.J.: Princeton University Press, 1956, pp. 94–116.

————. "The Spanish Tragedy." *Ernest Hemingway: Critiques of Four Major Novels.* Ed. Carlos Baker. New York: Charles Scribner's Sons, 1962, pp. 108–31.

Beatty, Sandra. "A Study of Female Characterization in Steinbeck's Fiction." *Steinbeck's Women: Essays in Criticism.* Ed. Tetsumaro Hayashi. Steinbeck Monograph Series, No. 9, 1979, pp. 1–6.

Bell, Millicent. "*A Farewell to Arms*: Pseudoautobiography and Personal Metaphor." *Ernest Hemingway: The Writer in Context.* Ed. James Nagel. Madison: University of Wisconsin Press, 1984, pp. 107–28.

Brocki, Sister Mary Damascene, CSSF. "Faulkner and Hemingway: Values in the Modern World." *Mark Twain Journal,* Summer, 1962, pp. 5–9, 15.

Brooks, Cleanth. "Primitivism in *The Sound and the Fury.*" *English Institute Essays 1952.* New York: Columbia University Press, 1954, pp. 5–28.

Burhans, Clinton S., Jr. "*The Old Man and the Sea*: Hemingway's Tragic Vision of Man." *Ernest Hemingway: Critiques of Four Major Novels.* Ed. Carlos Baker. New York: Charles Scribner's Sons, 1962, pp. 150–55.

Burnam, Tom. "Primitivism and Masculinity in the Works of Hemingway." *Modern Fiction Studies,* 1, No. 3 (August, 1955), 20–24.

Calisher, Hortense. "No Important Woman Writer." *Mademoiselle,* February 1970, pp. 188–89+.

Carlson, Eric W. "Symbolism in *The Grapes of Wrath.*" Reprinted in *A Casebook on The Grapes of Wrath.* Ed. Agnes McNeill Donohue. New York: Thomas Y. Crowell Company, 1968, pp. 96–102.

Carpenter, Frederick I. "The Philosophical Joads." Reprinted in *A Casebook on The Grapes of Wrath.* Ed. Agnes McNeill Donohue. New York: Thomas Y. Crowell Company, 1968, pp. 80–89.

Cass, Colin S. "The Love Story in *For Whom the Bell Tolls.*" *Fitzgerald/Hemingway Annual 1972.* pp. 225–35.

Chafetz, Morris E., M.D. "Alcoholism and Alcoholic Psychoses." *Comprehensive Textbook of Psychiatry/II.* Eds. Alfred M. Freedman, M.D., Harold I. Kaplan, M.D., Benjamin J. Sadock, M.D. Baltimore: The Williams & Wilkins Company, 1975, pp. 1331–48.

Chametzky, Jules. "The Ambivalent Endings of *The Grapes of Wrath.*" *Modern Fiction Studies,* 11 (Spring, 1965), 34–44.

Champney, Freeman. "John Steinbeck, Californian." *Steinbeck: A Collection of Critical Essays.* Ed. Robert Murray Davis. Englewood Cliffs, N.J.: Prentice-Hall, Inc., 1972, pp. 18–35.

Collins, Carvell. "A Note on *Sanctuary.*" *Harvard Advocate,* 135 (November 1951), 16.

———. "The Pairing of *The Sound and the Fury* and *As I Lay Dying.*" *Princeton University Library Chronicle,* 18 (Spring, 1957), 114–23.

———. "Nathanael West's *The Day of the Locust* and *Sanctuary.*" *Faulkner Studies,* 2 (Summer 1953), 23–24.

Cousins, Norman. "Hemingway and Steinbeck." *Saturday Review of Literature,* 28 October 1950, pp. 26–27.

Crockett, H. Kelley. "The Bible and *The Grapes of Wrath.*" Reprinted in *A Casebook on The Grapes of Wrath.* Ed. Agnes McNeill Donohue. New York: Thomas Y. Crowell Company, 1968, pp. 105–14.

Davidson, Arnold E. "The Ambivalent End of Francis Macomber's Short Happy Life." *Hemingway Notes,* 2, No. 1 (Spring, 1972), 14–16.

Detro, Gene. "Carol—The Woman behind the Man." *The Sunday Peninsula Herald Weekend Magazine.* 10 June 1984, pp. 3–6.

Ditsky, John. "Faulkner Land and Steinbeck Country." *Steinbeck: The Man and His Work.* Eds. Richard Astro and Tetsumaro Hayashi. Corvallis: Oregon State University Press, 1971, pp. 11–24.

_____. *Essays on East of Eden*. Muncie: The John Steinbeck Society of America, 1977. Steinbeck Monograph Series, No. 7.

Fisher, Deborah. "Genuine Heroines Hemingway Style." *Lost Generation Journal*, 2 (Spring-Summer 1974), 35–36.

Geismar, Maxwell. "To Have and to Have and to Have." *The Saturday Review of Literature*, 9 September 1950, p. 18.

_____. "A Rapt and Tumid Power." *The Saturday Review of Literature*, 12 July 1952, pp. 10–11.

Gilbert, Sandra. "Life Studies or Speech after Long Silence: Feminist Critics Today," *College English*, 40 (April, 1979), 849–63.

Greco, Anne. "Margot Macomber: 'Bitch Goddess,' Exonerated." *Fitzgerald/Hemingway Annual 1972.* pp. 273–79.

Gubar, Susan. "Mother, Maiden and the Marriage of Death: Women Writers and an Ancient Myth." *Women's Studies*, 6 (1979), 301–15.

Guttman, Allen. "Mechanized Doom." *Ernest Hemingway: Critiques of Four Major Novels*. Ed. Carlos Baker. New York: Charles Scribner's Sons, 1962, pp. 95–107.

Hamilton, Edith. "Faulkner: Sorcerer or Slave?" *The Saturday Review of Literature*, 12 July 1952, pp. 8–10, 39–41.

Hays, Peter L. "Exchange between Rivals: Faulkner's Influence on *The Old Man and the Sea*." *Ernest Hemingway: The Writer in Context*. Ed. James Nagel. Madison: University of Wisconsin Press, 1984, pp. 147–63.

Hedrick, Joan. "Mother Earth and Earth Mother: The Recasting of Myth in Steinbeck's *The Grapes of Wrath*." *The Grapes of Wrath: A Collection of Critical Essays*. Englewood Cliffs, N.J.: Prentice-Hall, 1982, pp. 134–45.

Heilbrun, Carolyn. "The Masculine Wilderness of the American Novel." *The Saturday Review of Literature*, 29 January 1972, pp. 41–44.

Hellstrom, Gustaf. "Presentation Address." *Nobel Prize Library*. New York: Alexis Gregory, 1971, pp. 3–6.

Jackson, Naomi. "Faulkner's Woman: Demon-Nun and Angel-Witch." *Ball State University Forum,* 8 (Winter, 1967), 12–20.

Kaufman, Donald L. "The Long Happy Life of Norman Mailer." *Modern Fiction Studies*, 17 (Autumn, 1971), 347–59.

Kent, George E. "The Black Woman in Faulkner's Works, with the Exclusion of Dilsey, Part I." *Phylon*, 35 (December, 1974), 430–41.

Kerr, Elizabeth M. "William Faulkner and the Southern Concept of Woman." *Mississippi Quarterly*, 15 (Winter, 1961–62), 1–16.

Kidd, Walter E. "Introduction." *American Winners of the Nobel Prize*. Eds. Walter E. Kidd and Warren G. French. Norman: University of Oklahoma Press, 1968, pp. 3–15.

Kindrick, Robert L. "Lizzie Dahlberg and Eula Varner: Two Modern Perspectives on the Earth Mother." *MidAmerica*, 2 (1975), 93–111.

Kobler, J.F. "Lena Grove: Faulkner's 'Still Unravish'd Bride of Quietness'." *Arizona Quarterly*, 28 (Winter, 1972), 339–54.

Latham, Aaron. "Unfinished Manuscripts Reveal a Hemingway No One Knew." *Chicago Tribune*, 17 October 1977, Sec. 3, p. 20.

Levin, Harry. "Observations on the Style of Ernest Hemingway." *Hemingway: A Collection of Critical Essays*. Ed. Robert P. Weeks. Englewood Cliffs, N.J.: Prentice-Hall, Inc., 1962, pp. 72–85.

Lind, Ilse Dusoir. "Faulkner's Women." *The Maker and The Myth: Faulkner and Yoknapatawpha 1977*. Eds. Evans Harrington and Ann J. Abadie. Jackson: University Press of Mississippi, 1978, pp. 89–104.

Linscott, Robert. "Faulkner without Fanfare." *Esquire*, 60 (July 1963), 38.

Lisca, Peter. "*The Grapes of Wrath* as Fiction." Reprinted in *A Casebook on The Grapes of Wrath*. Ed. Agnes McNeill Donohue. New York: Thomas Y. Crowell Company, 1968, pp. 166–81.

———. "Steinbeck's Image of Man and His Decline as a Writer." *Modern Fiction Studies*, 11 (Spring, 1965), 3–10.

Magny, Claude-Edmonde. "Book Review of John Steinbeck's *East of Eden*." Trans. Louise Varese. *Perspectives USA*, 5 (Fall, 1953), 146–49.

Martin, Wendy. "Seduced and Abandoned in the New World: The Fallen Woman in American Fiction." *Woman in Sexist Society*. Eds. Vivian Gornick and Barbara K. Moran. New York: New American Library, 1971, pp. 329–46.

McFarland, Holly. "The Mask Not Tragic...Just Damned: The Women in Faulkner's Trilogy." *Ball State University Forum*, 18 (1977), 27–50.

Miller, David M. "Faulkner's Women." *Modern Fiction Studies*, 13 (Spring, 1967), 3–17.

Moritz, Ken. "Ernest Hemingway." *American Winners of the Nobel Prize*. Eds. Warren G. French and Walter E. Kidd. Norman: University of Oklahoma Press, 1968, pp. 158–92.

Morris, Harry. "*The Pearl*: Realism and Allegory." *Steinbeck: A Collection of Critical Essays*. Ed. Robert Murray Davis. Englewood Cliffs, N.J.: Prentice-Hall, Inc., 1972, pp. 149–62.

Mortimer, Gail. "The Smooth, Suave Shape of Desire: Paradox in Faulkner's Imagery of Women." Forthcoming in *Women's Studies*.

Motley, Warren. "From Patriarchy to Matriarchy: Ma Joad's Role in *The Grapes of Wrath*." *American Literature*, 54 (October, 1982), 397–412.

Oldsey, Bernard. "Hemingway's Beginnings and Endings." *Ernest Hemingway: The Papers of a Writer*. New York: Garland Publishing Co., 1981, pp. 37–62.

Pearson, Janet Lynne. "Hemingway's Women." *Lost Generation Journal*, 1 (May, 1973), 16–19.

Plimpton, George. "The Art of Fiction XXI: Ernest Hemingway." *Paris Review*, Spring, 1958, pp. 60–89.

Pollock, Theodore. "On the Ending of *The Grapes of Wrath*." Reprinted in *A Casebook on The Grapes of Wrath*. Ed. Agnes McNeill Donohue. New York: Thomas J. Crowell Company, 1968, pp. 182–84.

Presley, John W. " 'Hawks Never Share:' Women and Tragedy in Hemingway." *Fitzgerald/Hemingway Annual 1973*. pp. 243–57.

Richards, Edmund C. " Challenge of John Steinbeck." *North American Review*, 243 (Summer, 1937), 406–13.

Rivlin, Lily. "Lilith: The First Woman." *MS*, December 1972, pp. 92–97, 114–15.

Schmidt, Dolores Barracano. "The Great American Bitch." *College English*, 32 (May, 1971), 900–905.

Shockley, Martin. "Christian Symbolism in *The Grapes of Wrath*." Reprinted in *A Casebook on The Grapes of Wrath*. Ed. Agnes McNeill Donohue. New York: Thomas Y. Crowell Company, 1968, pp. 90–95.

Smith, Carol H. "Women and the Loss of Eden in Hemingway's Mythology." *Ernest Hemingway: The Writer in Context*. Ed. James Nagel. Madison: University of Wisconsin Press, 1984, pp. 129–44.

Spilka, Mark. "Hemingway and Fauntleroy: An Androgynous Pursuit." *American Novelists Revisited: Essays in Feminist Criticism*. Boston: G.K. Hall & Co., 1982, pp. 339–70.

Stavn, Diane Gersoni. "Reducing the 'Miss Muffet' Syndrome: An Annotated Bibliography." *Library Journal*, 15 January 1972, pp. 256–59.

Steinbeck, John. "Acceptance Speech." *Nobel Prize Library*. New York: Alexis Gregory, 1971.

Stonesifer, Richard. "In Defense of Dewey Dell." *Educational Leader*, 22 (July, 1958), 27–33.

Tuttleton, James W. " 'Combat in the Erogenous Zone': Women in the American Novel between the Two World Wars." *What Manner of Woman.* Ed. Marlene Springer. New York: New York University Press, 1977, pp. 271–96.

van den Haag, Ernest. "How Now Kate." *National Review*, 22 (22 September 1970), 1004–05.

Wagner, Linda W. " ' Proud and Friendly and Gently': Women in Hemingway's Early Fiction." *Ernest Hemingway: The Papers of a Writer.* Ed. Bernard Oldsey. New York: Garland Publishing, Inc., 1981, pp. 63–72.

Weinstein, Philip. "Meditations on the Other: Faulkner's Rendering of Women." Forthcoming in *Faulkner and Women: Faulkner and Yoknapatawpha 1985.*

Weisstein, Naomi. "Stimulus/Response: Woman as Nigger." *Psychology Today*, 3 (October, 1969) 20–22, 58.

Westbrook, Max. "Grace under Pressure: Hemingway and the Summer of 1920." *Ernest Hemingway: The Writer in Context.* Ed. James Nagel. Madison: University of Wisconsin Press, 1984, pp. 77–106.

Wilson, Edmund. "Ernest Hemingway." *Atlantic Monthly*, July, 1939, pp. 36–46.

————. "Hemingway: Gauge of Morale." *The Wound and the Bow* (Oxford: Oxford University Press, 1947). Reprinted in *Ernest Hemingway: The Man and His Work.* Ed. John K. M. McCaffery. New York: World Publishing Company, 1950, pp. 236–57.

Wittenberg, Judith Bryant. "William Faulkner: A Feminist Consideration." *American Novelists Revisited: Essays in Feminist Criticism.* Boston: G.K. Hall & Co., 1982, pp. 325–38.

Wright, Celest Turner. "Ancient Analogues of an Incident in John Steinbeck." Reprinted in *A Casebook on The Grapes of Wrath.* Ed. Agnes McNeill Donohue. New York: Thomas Y. Crowell Company, 1968, pp. 159–61.

Index